Elementary Poetry
Textbook and Activity Book
by Sonja Glumich

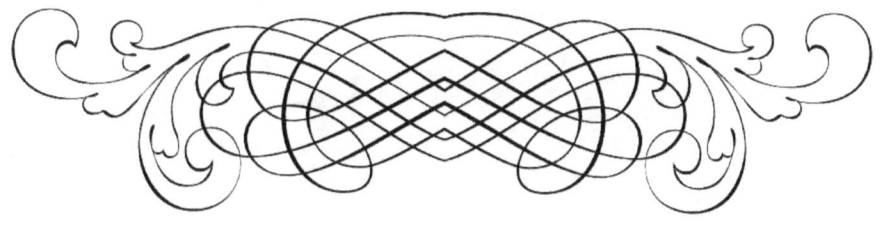

Poetry Study for Elementary School-Aged Children

Volume 4: Advancing in Poetry

Interweaves poetry, vocabulary, mapwork, discussion, copywork, narration, and dictation.

Under the Home Press Division
www.underthehome.org

Front Cover
Little Girl Chasing Butterflies
Image by Jill Wellington
CC0 Creative Commons ({PD-US})
original source: *pixabay.com/en/chasing-butterflies-little-girl-2516581/*

Copyright © 2018 Sonja Glumich
All rights reserved.

No part of this work may be reproduced, scanned, or electronically transmitted without prior permission of the copyright owner unless actions are expressly permitted by federal law the family exception detailed below.

The copyright owner grants an exception for photocopying or scanning and printing pages for use within an immediate family only. Scanned pages should never be used for any other purpose including sharing between families, posting online, transmitting electronically, or resale.

This exception does not extend to schools or co-ops, however a reasonable licensing fee for reproduction can be negotiated by contacting Under the Home, the publisher.

For more information or to report errata, please contact Under the Home at contact@underthehome.org.

ISBN: 1948783002
ISBN-13: 978-1948783002

DEDICATION

For Chris, Everett, Cassidy, and Calista – my beloved family and curricula test squad.

TABLE OF CONTENTS

POET I: EMILY DICKINSON
Lesson 1. I'm Nobody! Who are you? 1
Lesson 2. Hope is the Thing with Feathers 8
Lesson 3. Because I Could Not Stop for Death 14
Lesson 4. By the Sea 20

POET II: ROBERT FROST
Lesson 5. After Apple-Picking 26
Lesson 6. Ghost House 33
Lesson 7. October 39
Lesson 8. The Lockless Door 44

POET III: HENRY WADSWORTH LONGFELLOW
Lesson 9. Haunted Houses 49
Lesson 10. Paul Revere's Ride 58
Lesson 11. The Tide Rises, the Tide Falls 68
Lesson 12. Snow-flakes 74

POET IV: PAUL LAURENCE DUNBAR
Lesson 13. We Wear the Mask 80
Lesson 14. The Seedling 87
Lesson 15. Sunset 93
Lesson 16. He Had His Dream 99

POET V: CHRISTINA GEORGINA ROSSETTI
Lesson 17. A Birthday 105
Lesson 18. Uphill 113
Lesson 19. The Queen of Hearts 119
Lesson 20. Summer 126

POET VI: AMY LOWELL
Lesson 21. The Travelling Bear 132
Lesson 22. To a Friend 139
Lesson 23. Venus Transiens 145
Lesson 24. Winter's Turning 151

POET VII: JOHN KEATS
Lesson 25. Bright Star, would I were steadfast as thou art 157
Lesson 26. Ode to Autumn 164
Lesson 27. On the Grasshopper and Cricket 172
Lesson 28. To Sleep 177

POET VIII: WALT WHITMAN
Lesson 29. A Noiseless Patient Spider 183
Lesson 30. Longings for Home 190
Lesson 31. Night on the Prairies 197
Lesson 32. Pioneers! O Pioneers! 203

POET IX: ELIZABETH BARRETT BROWNING
Lesson 33. How Do I Love Thee?...212
Lesson 34. The Best Thing in the World..219
Lesson 35. The Musical Instrument...224
Lesson 36. Change Upon Change..230

MINI DICTIONARY..235

REFERENCES AND ADDITIONAL READING...248

Goals of This Book Series

This book series aims to familiarize children with works of poetry from an early age, nurture the imagination, inspire an appreciation for beauty, encourage a mind for symbolism and nuance, foster the ability to narrate and dictate complex ideas, and expand children's vocabularies and geographical knowledge. Lessons are short and interactive by design to target elementary school-aged children.

Inspiration for This Book Series

Charlotte Mason, born in 1842, sought to provide teaching advice and strategies to instructors and homeschooling parents. She detailed her educational philosophies and methodologies in her multi-volume *Home Education Series*. She advocated for centering instruction around living works, such as the finest art, music, poetry, and prose. Mason recommended that from an early age, children engage in the regular study of poetry, including reciting poetry. In her *Home Education Series*, she writes, "…include a good deal of poetry, to accustom him to the delicate rendering of shades of meaning, and especially to make him aware that words are beautiful in themselves, that they are a source of pleasure, and are worthy of our honour; and that a beautiful word deserves to be beautifully said, with a certain roundness of tone and precision of utterance."

The Targeted Audience for This Book

This book targets elementary school-aged children ages eight and up.

Overview of This Book

This book provides 36 lessons, or enough for one lesson per week over a standard 36-week school year. This volume highlights nine master poets and their poetry. Children study four poems by each poet with one new poem introduced weekly. The selected poems in this book appeal to children and their adult instructors by featuring nature, animals, friendship, the seasons, emotions, mystery, trials, and triumphs. Lessons also introduce the concept of literary devices such as metaphors, similes, and personification.

This volume features the following poets:
- Emily Dickinson
- Robert Frost
- Henry Wadsworth Longfellow
- Paul Laurence Dunbar
- Christina Rossetti
- Amy Lowell
- John Keats
- Walt Whitman
- Elizabeth Barrett Browning

How to Teach Using This Book

The tables below outline the recommended instructional approach to teach a 36-week course using this book.

Every Four Weeks – Introduce a New Poet	
Section Title	**Section Instructions**
Poet Overview	Instructors and students read and discuss the biographical information of the poet.
Color the Poet	Students color the portrait of the poet.
Map the Poet	Students find and color geographical locations related to the poet.

Every Week – Introduce a New Poem	
Section Title	**Section Instructions**
Featured Poem	• Students practice reciting the poem. • Students may color poem illustrations as desired.
Synopsis	Instructors and students review the synopsis of the poem.
Recite Poem Information	Students practice reciting the poem title and the name of the poet.
Study Poem Pictures	Students describe how the included pictures relate to the poem.
Vocabulary	• Students practice pronouncing the featured vocabulary words. • Students copy the vocabulary words. • Students copy definitions from the mini dictionary at the end of the book.
Narrate the Poem	Students write a summary of the poem in their own words.
Copy the Excerpt	Students copy the provided poem excerpt.
Narrate the Excerpt	Students write a summary of the excerpt in their own words.
Dictate the Excerpt	Instructors recite the excerpt, and children write the words as they are spoken.
Draw the Poem	Students create novel artwork visually representing how they experience the poem.

ELEMENTARY POETRY VOLUME 4: ADVANCING IN POETRY

POET I: EMILY DICKINSON
LESSON 1. "I'M NOBODY! WHO ARE YOU?"

POET OVERVIEW

- Emily Dickinson was born in 1830 in Amherst, Massachusetts.
- Dickinson was solitary and reclusive throughout her life.
- Dickinson never married and retreated from the rest of the world to regularly stay in her bedroom.
- Dickinson did not achieve acclaim for her poetry during her life, publishing less than a dozen poems.
- Dickinson's younger sister found hundreds of previously unknown poems after her death, which were eventually published to great acclaim.
- Dickinson died of Bright's disease in Amherst, Massachusetts at the age of 55.

COLOR THE POET

MAP THE POET

Locate and color Dickinson's state of birth, **Massachusetts (MA)**, on the map of the United States.

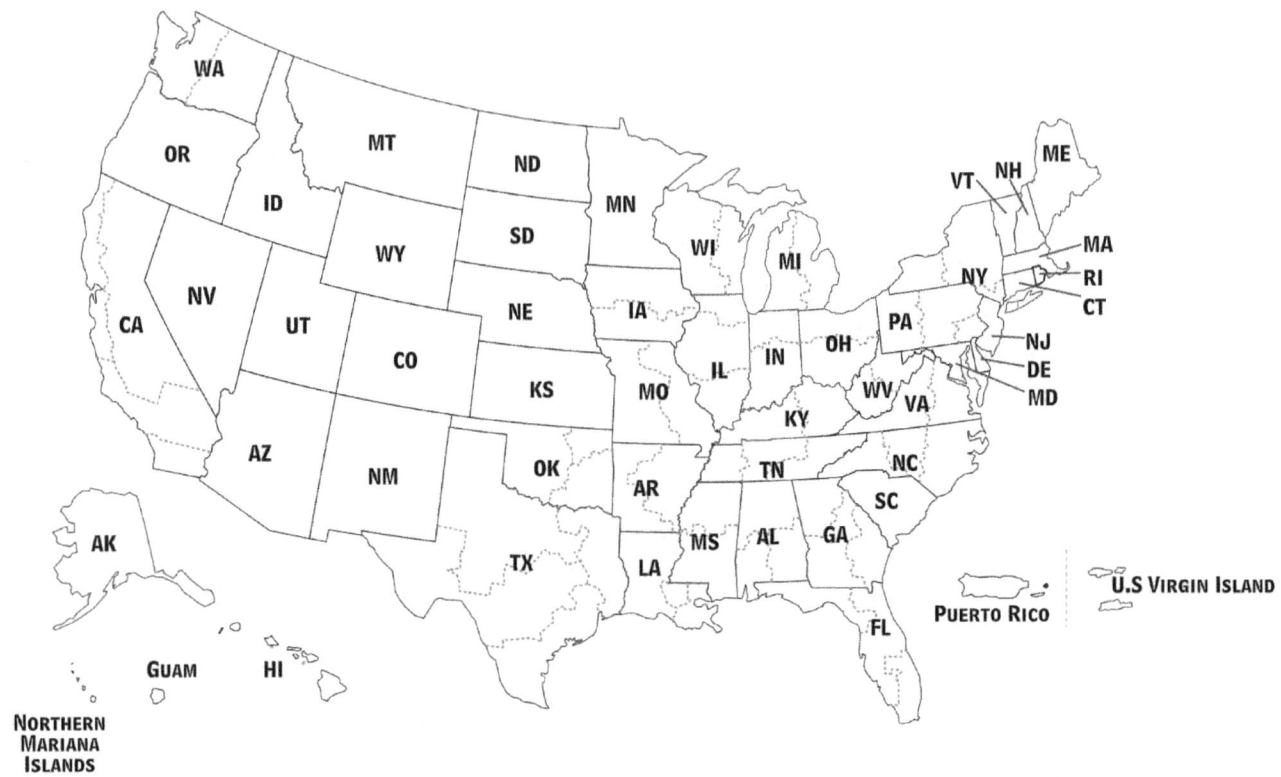

FEATURED POEM

I'm Nobody! Who are you?

Are you – Nobody – too?

Then there's a pair of us!

Don't tell! they'd advertise – you know!

How dreary – to be – Somebody!

How public – like a Frog –

To tell your name – the livelong June –

To an admiring Bog!

ELEMENTARY POETRY VOLUME 4: ADVANCING IN POETRY

SYNOPSIS

Emily Dickinson's "I'm Nobody! Who are you?" presents a fun conundrum. How can "Nobody" narrate a poem and ask the reader questions? "Nobody" may refer to what others think of the narrator rather than a state of being. Perhaps a hidden word follows, such as "Nobody Important" or "Nobody Famous" or "Nobody Notorious." The narrator claims to favor their anonymity, comparing "Somebodies" to a bunch of frogs ceaselessly croaking to their star-struck, marsh-inhabiting followers.

ENRICHMENT ACTIVITIES

1. **Recite Poem Information**
   Recite the title of the poem, the name of the poet, and the poem.

2. **Study the Poem Picture**
   Study the poem pictures, and describe how they relate to the poem.

3. **Discuss Introversion and Extroversion**
   - Have you ever heard of introverts and extroverts?
   - Introverts prefer small gatherings of friends and family and having ample alone time to recharge.
   - Extroverts love spending time with both their families and big groups of people. They gain energy being out and about and socializing with the world.
   - Some people are very introverted, some have traits of both introverts and extroverts, and others are very extroverted.
   - Do you think Emily Dickinson was more of an introvert or an extrovert? Explain why.
   - Do you think you are an introvert, an extrovert, or a mixture of the two? Explain why.

VOCABULARY (Students copy definitions from the mini dictionary at the end of the book.)

Recite and Copy Each Word	Write the Definition
nobody *nobody*	*1. No person; no one.* *2. A person of no importance or authority.*
pair	
advertise	
dreary	

Recite and Copy Each Word	Write the Definition
somebody	
livelong	
public	
admiring	
bog	

NARRATE THE POEM (Students write a summary of the poem in their own words.)

COPY THE EXCERPT (Students copy the provided poem excerpt.)

I'm Nobody! Who are you?
Are you – Nobody – too?

NARRATE THE EXCERPT (Students write a summary of the excerpt in their own words.)

_____

_____

_____

_____

_____

_____

DICTATE THE EXCERPT (Instructors recite the excerpt, and students write the words.)

_____

_____

_____

_____

_____

DRAW THE POEM (Students create a visual representation of the poem.)

Poem Title:	Poem Author:

LESSON 2. "HOPE IS THE THING WITH FEATHERS" BY EMILY DICKINSON

FEATURED POEM

Hope is the thing with feathers,

That perches in the soul,

And sings the tune without the words,

And never stops at all,

And sweetest in the gale is heard,

And sore must be the storm,

That could abash the little bird

That kept so many warm.

I've heard it in the chillest land,

And on the strangest Sea;

Yet, never, in extremity,

It asked a crumb of me.

SYNOPSIS

Emily Dickinson's "Hope is the Thing with Feathers" employs a feathered, soul-perching, singing, and ceaseless bird as a metaphor for hope. Imagine in your head, the inspiring sight of every person walking around with a little bird perched upon their soul, singing and inspiring us to keep trying in our darkest times.

ENRICHMENT ACTIVITIES

1. **Recite Poem Information**
   Recite the title of the poem, the name of the poet, and the poem.

2. **Study the Poem Picture**
   Study the poem picture, and describe how it relates to the poem.

3. **Create Your Own Metaphors**
   - In this poem, Dickinson employs a literary device called a metaphor.
   - A metaphor uses a word or phrase to refer to something that it is not to make an implied comparison.
   - This poem employs a perching bird as a metaphor for hope.
   - Study the examples of metaphors:
     - The snow was a white curtain.
     - The classroom was a zoo.
     - His heart was a galloping stallion.
     - Her eyes were two shining stars.
     - He was a skeleton.
     - The kitty's fur was a warm winter coat.
     - The fire was a raging beast.
     - The house was a cage.
     - His feet are canoes.
   - Fill in the blanks to create your own metaphors:

     Her cheeks were two red _____.

     My bedroom is a _____.

     _____ is a sharp dagger.

     His elbows are two pointed _____.

     _____ is a warm hug.

VOCABULARY (Students copy definitions from the mini dictionary at the end of the book.)

Recite and Copy Each Word	Write the Definition
hope	
perches	
soul	
tune	
gale	
abash	
chillest	
strangest	
extremity	
metaphor	

NARRATE THE POEM (Students write a summary of the poem in their own words.)

_____

_____

_____

_____

_____

_____

COPY THE EXCERPT (Students copy the provided poem excerpt.)

Hope is the thing with feathers,
That perches in the soul

_____

_____

_____

_____

NARRATE THE EXCERPT (Students write a summary of the excerpt in their own words.)

DICTATE THE EXCERPT (Instructors recite the excerpt, and students write the words.)

ELEMENTARY POETRY VOLUME 4: ADVANCING IN POETRY

DRAW THE POEM (Students create a visual representation of the poem.)

Poem Title:	Poem Author:

LESSON 3. "BECAUSE I COULD NOT STOP FOR DEATH" BY EMILY DICKINSON

FEATURED POEM

1. Because I could not stop for Death,

He kindly stopped for me;

The carriage held but just ourselves

And Immortality.

2. We slowly drove, he knew no haste,

And I had put away

My labor, and my leisure too,

For his civility.

3. We passed the school where children played,

Their lessons scarcely done;

We passed the fields of gazing grain,

We passed the setting sun.

4. We paused before a house that seemed

A swelling of the ground;

The roof was scarcely visible,

The cornice but a mound.

5. Since then 'tis centuries; but each

Feels shorter than the day

I first surmised the horses' heads

Were toward eternity.

SYNOPSIS

Emily Dickinson's "Because I Could Not Stop for Death" ("The Chariot") depicts death as a dignified gentleman driving a carriage and kindly collecting the narrator before embarking on a leisurely drive toward eternity. On the way, they see children enjoying recess at school, fields of grain, the setting sun, and a strangely sunken house. Time flows differently during the carriage ride. A day in death's carriage lasts centuries in the human world.

ENRICHMENT ACTIVITIES

1. **Recite Poem Information**
   Recite the title of the poem, the name of the poet, and the poem.

2. **Study the Poem Pictures**
   Study the poem pictures, and describe how they relate to the poem.

3. **Discuss the Poem**
   - Death may be an unsettling concept to ponder or discuss.
   - What does this poem make you think about?
   - How does reading this poem make you feel?

VOCABULARY (Students copy definitions from the mini dictionary at the end of the book.)

Recite and Copy Each Word	Write the Definition
carriage	
immortality	
haste	
labor	
leisure	
civility	

Recite and Copy Each Word	Write the Definition
strove	
scarcely	
visible	
cornice	
centuries	
surmised	
eternity	

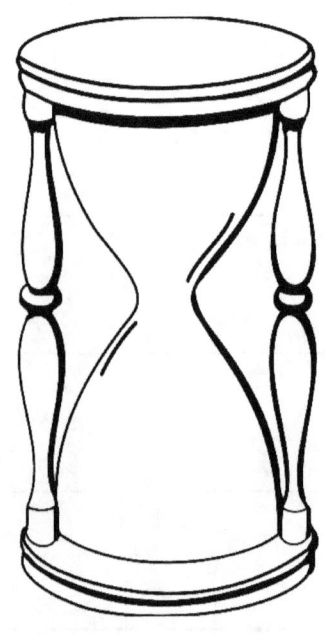

NARRATE THE POEM (Students write a summary of the poem in their own words.)

COPY THE EXCERPT (Students copy the provided poem excerpt.)

The Carriage held but just Ourselves —
And Immortality.

NARRATE THE EXCERPT (Students write a summary of the excerpt in their own words.)

DICTATE THE EXCERPT (Instructors recite the excerpt, and students write the words.)

DRAW THE POEM (Students create a visual representation of the poem.)

Poem Title:	Poem Author:

SONJA GLUMICH

LESSON 4. "BY THE SEA" BY EMILY DICKINSON

FEATURED POEM

1. I started Early, took my Dog,

And visited the Sea;

The Mermaids in the Basement

Came out to look at me.

2. And Frigates – in the Upper Floor

Extended Hempen Hands –

Presuming Me to be a Mouse –

Aground – upon the Sands –

3. But no Man moved Me – till the Tide

Went past my simple Shoe –

And past my Apron – and my Belt

And past my Bodice – too –

4. And made as He would eat me up –

As wholly as a Dew

Upon a Dandelion's Sleeve –

And then – I started – too –

5. And He – He followed – close behind –

I felt His Silver Heel

Upon my Ankle – Then My Shoes

Would overflow with Pearl –

6. Until We met the Solid Town –

No Man He seemed to know –

And bowing – with a Mighty look –

At me – The Sea withdrew –

SYNOPSIS

Emily Dickinson's "By the Sea" describes a girl and her dog taking an early morning stroll along the sea. The tide eventually rises and drives her away. In stanzas one and two, the sea is a house with mermaids in the basement (under the water) and sailors upstairs (above the water). For the remaining stanzas, as the tide rises, the sea becomes a man who threatens to drown the narrator and chases her back to town.

ENRICHMENT ACTIVITIES

1. **Recite Poem Information**
   Recite the title of the poem, the name of the poet, and the poem.

2. **Study the Poem Pictures**
   Study the poem pictures, and describe they relate to the poem.

3. **Discuss the Poem**
   - How does this poem reflect on the changing and complex nature of the sea?
   - What do you imagine when you consider our vast seas?
   - How can the sea be fun?
   - How can the sea be inspiring?
   - How can the sea be frightening?

4. **Discuss Personification**
   - In this poem, Dickinson employs a literary device called personification.
   - Personification assigns human qualities to inanimate objects or ideas.
   - Study the three poem excerpts, and explain why each offers an example of personification:
     o And made as He would eat me up –
     o And He – He followed – close behind
     o And bowing – with a Mighty look – At me – The Sea withdrew;

VOCABULARY (Students copy definitions from the mini dictionary at the end of the book.)

Recite and Copy Each Word	Write the Definition
frigates	
extended	
hempen	
presuming	
aground	
tide	
bodice	
dew	
overflow	
withdrew	

NARRATE THE POEM (Students write a summary of the poem in their own words.)

_____

_____

_____

_____

_____

_____

COPY THE EXCERPT (Students copy the provided poem excerpt.)

I started early, took my dog,
And visited the sea;
The mermaids in the basement
Came out to look at me.

_____

_____

_____

_____

NARRATE THE EXCERPT (Students write a summary of the excerpt in their own words.)

DICTATE THE EXCERPT (Instructors recite the excerpt, and students write the words.)

DRAW THE POEM (Students create a visual representation of the poem.)

Poem Title:	Poem Author:

POET II: ROBERT FROST
LESSON 5. "AFTER APPLE-PICKING"

POET OVERVIEW

- Robert Frost was born in 1874 in San Francisco, California.
- Frost moved to Massachusetts at age eleven when his father died of tuberculosis.
- Frost's time spent in New England inspired his poetry.
- Frost worked many jobs including as a factory worker, a farmer, a school teacher, and a college professor, but always believed his true calling was that of a poet.
- Frost married and had six children, although many of the children died young and only two outlived their father.
- Frost died of a heart attack in Boston, Massachusetts at the age of 88.

COLOR THE POET

MAP THE POET

Locate and color Frost's state of birth, **California (CA)**, on the map of the United States. Trace his path when he moved to **Massachusetts (MA)**. Color **Massachusetts (MA)** a different color.

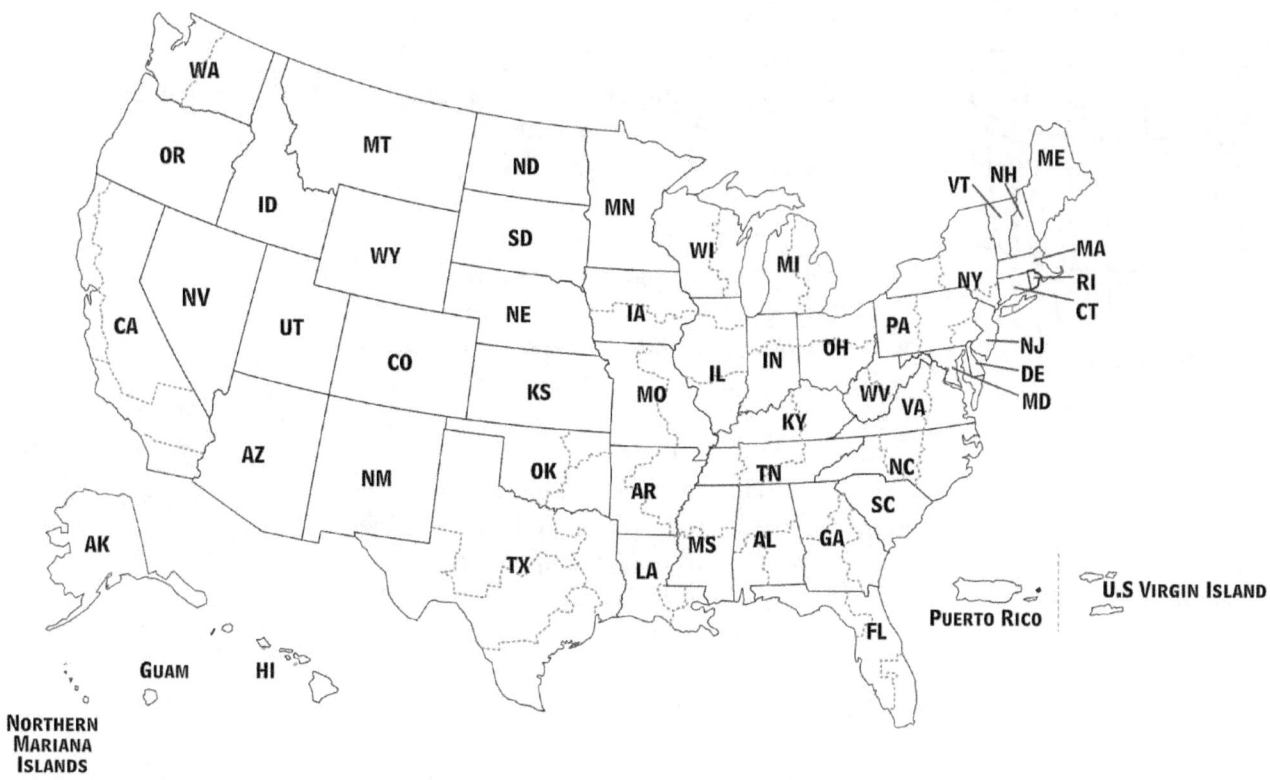

FEATURED POEM

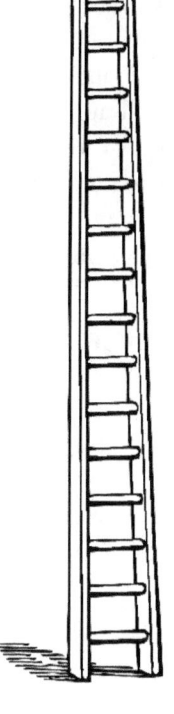

My long two-pointed ladder's sticking through a tree
Toward heaven still,
And there's a barrel that I didn't fill
Beside it, and there may be two or three

Apples I didn't pick upon some bough.
But I am done with apple-picking now.
Essence of winter sleep is on the night,
The scent of apples: I am drowsing off.

I cannot rub the strangeness from my sight
I got from looking through a pane of glass
I skimmed this morning from the drinking trough
And held against the world of hoary grass.

It melted, and I let it fall and break.
But I was well
Upon my way to sleep before it fell,
And I could tell
What form my dreaming was about to take.

Magnified apples appear and disappear,
Stem end and blossom end,
And every fleck of russet showing clear.
My instep arch not only keeps the ache,

It keeps the pressure of a ladder-round.
I feel the ladder sway as the boughs bend.
And I keep hearing from the cellar bin
The rumbling sound
Of load on load of apples coming in.

For I have had too much
Of apple-picking: I am overtired
Of the great harvest I myself desired.
There were ten thousand thousand fruit to touch,
Cherish in hand, lift down, and not let fall.

For all
That struck the earth,
No matter if not bruised or spiked with stubble,
Went surely to the cider-apple heap
As of no worth.
One can see what will trouble

This sleep of mine, whatever sleep it is.
Were he not gone,
The woodchuck could say whether it's like his
Long sleep, as I describe its coming on,
Or just some human sleep.

SYNOPSIS

In Robert Frost's "After Apple-Picking," a laborer is exhausted after a long season of picking apples. There are still apples waiting to be picked off trees and an empty barrel, but the laborer is too tired to care. The image of apples, the feeling of standing on a swaying ladder, and the rumbling sound of tumbling apples haunts the laborer's mind as he drifts off to sleep. As winter is approaching, the woodchuck has disappeared into its winter burrow, so the laborer cannot ask whether his sleep will be a groundhog-like hibernation or just a normal human slumber.

ENRICHMENT ACTIVITIES

1. **Recite Poem Information**
   Recite the title of the poem, the name of the poet, and the poem.

2. **Study the Poem Pictures**
   Study the poem pictures, and describe how they relate to the poem.

3. **Discuss the Poem**
    - Have you ever done something all day that haunts your mind as you fall asleep? Perhaps you swam all day and saw waves as you closed your tired eyes.
    - Have you ever picked apples off a tree, drank apple cider, or ate apple pie, apple crisp, or apple dumplings?
    - Have you ever felt so tired, you imagined you might hibernate in a burrow of blankets, like a groundhog in an earthen burrow?

VOCABULARY (Students copy definitions from the mini dictionary at the end of the book.)

Recite and Copy Each Word	Write the Definition
beside	
bough	
essence	
drowsing	
trough	
hoary	
russet	
instep	
stubble	

NARRATE THE POEM (Students write a summary of the poem in their own words.)

_____

_____

_____

_____

_____

_____

COPY THE EXCERPT (Students copy the provided poem excerpt.)

My instep arch not only keeps the ache,
It keeps the pressure of a ladder-round.

_____

_____

_____

_____

NARRATE THE EXCERPT (Students write a summary of the excerpt in their own words.)

DICTATE THE EXCERPT (Instructors recite the excerpt, and students write the words.)

DRAW THE POEM (Students create a visual representation of the poem.)

Poem Title:	Poem Author:

ELEMENTARY POETRY VOLUME 4: ADVANCING IN POETRY

LESSON 6. "GHOST HOUSE" BY ROBERT FROST

FEATURED POEM

1. I dwell in a lonely house I know

That vanished many a summer ago,

And left no trace but the cellar walls,

And a cellar in which the daylight falls

And the purple-stemmed wild raspberries grow.

2. O'er ruined fences the grape-vines shield

The woods come back to the mowing field;

The orchard tree has grown one copse

Of new wood and old where the woodpecker chops;

The footpath down to the well is healed.

3. I dwell with a strangely aching heart

In that vanished abode there far apart

On that disused and forgotten road

That has no dust-bath now for the toad.

Night comes; the black bats tumble and dart;

4. The whippoorwill is coming to shout

And hush and cluck and flutter about:

I hear him begin far enough away

Full many a time to say his say

Before he arrives to say it out.

5. It is under the small, dim, summer star.

I know not who these mute folk are

Who share the unlit place with me—

Those stones out under the low-limbed tree

Doubtless bear names that the mosses mar.

6. They are tireless folk, but slow and sad—

Though two, close-keeping, are lass and lad,—

With none among them that ever sings,

And yet, in view of how many things,

As sweet companions as might be had.

SYNOPSIS

In Robert Frost's "Ghost House," a ghostly narrator describes his home, a cellar shell of a house long forgotten by living people. Nature slowly reclaims the abandoned property - the top of the house is gone and vegetation overgrows the fences, footpath, and road. The narrator's only companions are bats, birds, and the long ago buried folks whose tombstone-engraved names are obscured by moss.

ENRICHMENT ACTIVITIES

1. **Recite Poem Information**
   Recite the title of the poem, the name of the poet, and the poem.

2. **Study the Poem Picture**
   Study the poem picture, and describe how it relates to the poem.

3. **Find the Lines**
   Find the lines in the poem that:
   - Tell the reader the narrator is deceased.
   - Tell the reader the ghost house is near a cemetery.
   - Are sad.
   - Are hopeful.
   - Describe plants.
   - Describe animals.

VOCABULARY (Students copy definitions from the mini dictionary at the end of the book.)

Recite and Copy Each Word	Write the Definition
dwell	
vanished	
trace	
cellar	
o'er	

Recite and Copy Each Word	Write the Definition
copse	
abode	
disused	
whippoorwill	
mute	
doubtless	
mar	
tireless	
lass	
lad	
companions	

NARRATE THE POEM (Students write a summary of the poem in their own words.)

_____

_____

_____

_____

_____

_____

_____

COPY THE EXCERPT (Students copy the provided poem excerpt.)

I dwell in a lonely house I know
That vanished many a summer ago,
And left no trace but the cellar walls,
And a cellar in which the daylight falls

_____

_____

_____

_____

_____

NARRATE THE EXCERPT (Students write a summary of the excerpt in their own words.)

DICTATE THE EXCERPT (Instructors recite the excerpt, and students write the words.)

DRAW THE POEM (Students create a visual representation of the poem.)

Poem Title:	Poem Author:

LESSON 7. "OCTOBER"
BY ROBERT FROST

FEATURED POEM

O hushed October morning mild,
Thy leaves have ripened to the fall;
Tomorrow's wind, if it be wild,
Should waste them all.
The crows above the forest call;
Tomorrow they may form and go.
O hushed October morning mild,
Begin the hours of this day slow,
Make the day seem to us less brief.
Hearts not averse to being beguiled,
Beguile us in the way you know;
Release one leaf at break of day;
At noon release another leaf;
One from our trees, one far away;
Retard the sun with gentle mist;
enshade the land with amethyst.
Slow, slow!
For the grapes' sake, if they were all,
Whose leaves already are burnt with frost,
Whose clustered fruit must else be lost—
For the grapes' sake along the wall.

SYNOPSIS

Robert Frost's "October" describes the sights, sounds, and delights of the autumn month of October. The narrator asks October to beguile us and to move slowly to avoid spoiling the grapes before they can be harvested.

ENRICHMENT ACTIVITIES

1. **Recite Poem Information**
   Recite the title of the poem, the name of the poet, and the poem.

2. **Study the Poem Pictures**
   Study the poem pictures, and describe how they relate to the poem.

3. **Find the Lines**
   Find the lines in the poem that ask October to:
   - Enchant us.
   - Shield the sun with mist.
   - Slow the cold and frost to allow the grapes to be picked before they are ruined.

VOCABULARY (Students copy definitions from the mini dictionary at the end of the book.)

Recite and Copy Each Word	Write the Definition
hushed	
waste	
averse	
beguile	
enchant	
amethyst	

NARRATE THE POEM (Students write a summary of the poem in their own words.)

COPY THE EXCERPT (Students copy the provided poem excerpt.)

Retard the sun with gentle mist;
Enchant the land with amethyst.

NARRATE THE EXCERPT (Students write a summary of the excerpt in their own words.)

DICTATE THE EXCERPT (Instructors recite the excerpt, and students write the words.)

DRAW THE POEM (Students create a visual representation of the poem.)

Poem Title:	Poem Author:

SONJA GLUMICH

LESSON 8. "THE LOCKLESS DOOR" BY ROBERT FROST

FEATURED POEM

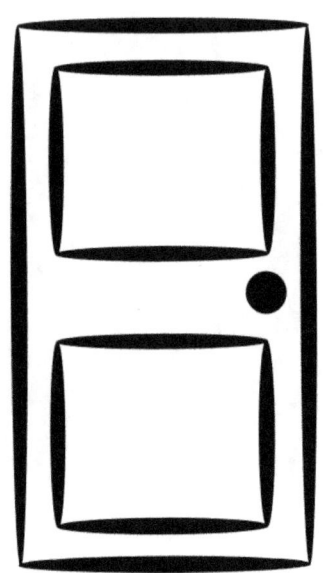

It went many years,
But at last came a knock,
And I thought of the door
With no lock to lock.

I blew out the light,
I tip-toed the floor,
And raised both hands
In prayer to the door.

But the knock came again
My window was wide;
I climbed on the sill
And descended outside.

Back over the sill
I bade a "Come in"
To whoever the knock
At the door may have been.

So at a knock
I emptied my cage
To hide in the world
And alter with age.

SYNOPSIS

In Robert Frost's "The Lockless Door," the narrator lives the life of a hermit, tucked away from the world within a refuge that has no visitors and needs no lock...until the day a knock sounds at the door. The narrator climbs out the window and stands outside before calling, "Come in," through the window. Just one knock changes the narrator's refuge into a hostile land and the outside hostile land into his refuge.

ENRICHMENT ACTIVITIES

1. **Recite Poem Information**
   Recite the title of the poem, the name of the poet, and the poem.

2. **Study the Poem Pictures**
   Study the poem pictures, and describe how they relate to the poem.

3. **Find the Lines**
   Find the lines in the poem where:
   - Someone knocks on the door.
   - The narrator climbs out the window.
   - The narrator realizes his sanctuary has become dangerous and the outside world has become his sanctuary.

VOCABULARY (Students copy definitions from the mini dictionary at the end of the book.)

Recite and Copy Each Word	Write the Definition
prayer	
wide	
sill	
descended	
cage	
alter	

NARRATE THE POEM (Students write a summary of the poem in their own words.)

COPY THE EXCERPT (Students copy the provided poem excerpt.)

I blew out the light,
I tip-toed the floor,
And raised both hands
In prayer to the door.

NARRATE THE EXCERPT (Students write a summary of the excerpt in their own words.)

DICTATE THE EXCERPT (Instructors recite the excerpt, and students write the words.)

DRAW THE POEM (Students create a visual representation of the poem.)

Poem Title:	Poem Author:

ELEMENTARY POETRY VOLUME 4: ADVANCING IN POETRY

POET III: HENRY WADSWORTH LONGFELLOW
LESSON 9. "HAUNTED HOUSES"

POET OVERVIEW

- Henry Wadsworth Longfellow was born in 1807 in Portland, Maine.
- Longfellow's ancestors included pilgrims who came to America from England on the Mayflower.
- Longfellow's grandfather was a general in the American Revolutionary War and a congressman.
- Longfellow was an avid student who loved learning and reading.
- In his life, Longfellow married, had six children, toured Europe, worked as a college professor, and became a well-known poet.
- Longfellow was part of a group of five New England poets called the "Fireside Poets."
- Longfellow died of peritonitis in Cambridge, Massachusetts at the age of 75.

COLOR THE POET

MAP THE POET

Locate and color Longfellow's state of birth, **Maine (ME)**, and state of death, **Massachusetts (MA)**, on the map of the United States.

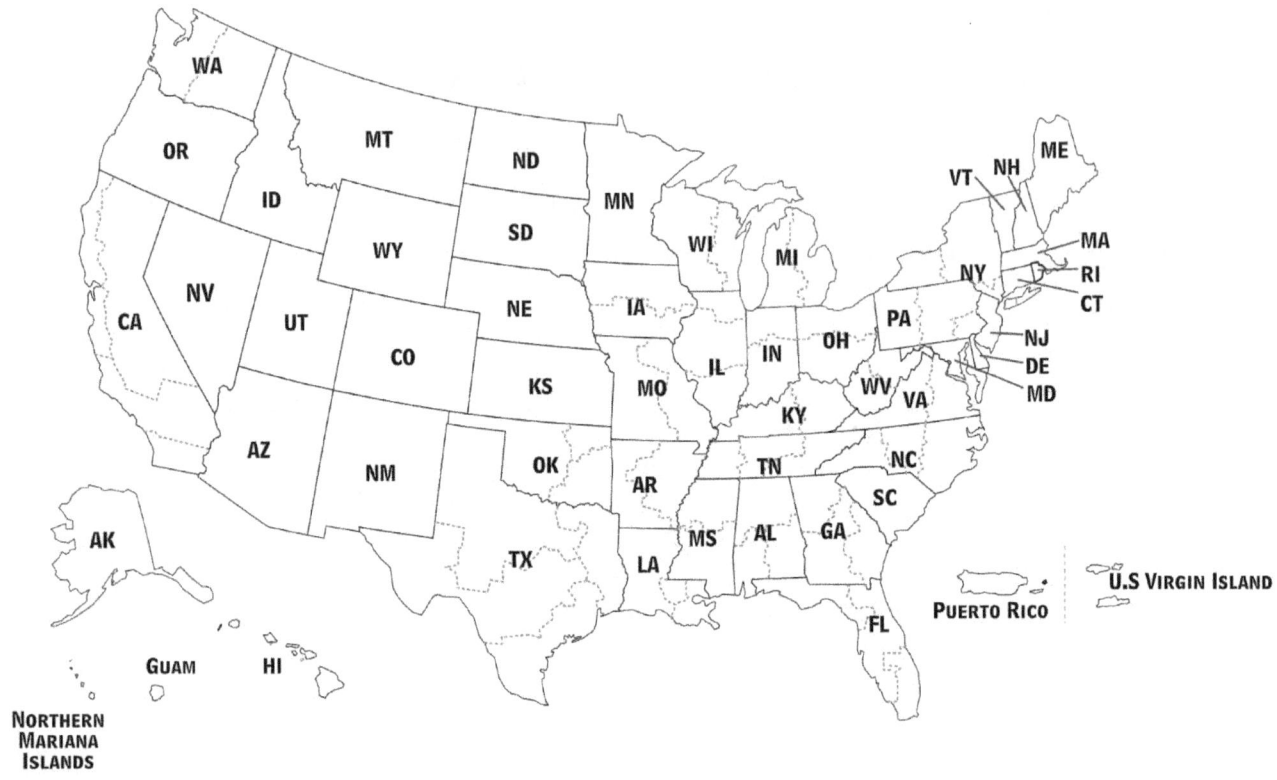

FEATURED POEM

All houses wherein men have lived and died
Are haunted houses. Through the open doors
The harmless phantoms on their errands glide,
With feet that make no sound upon the floors.

We meet them at the doorway, on the stair,
Along the passages they come and go,
Impalpable impressions on the air,
A sense of something moving to and fro.

There are more guests at table than the hosts
Invited; the illuminated hall
Is thronged with quiet, inoffensive ghosts,
As silent as the pictures on the wall.

The stranger at my fireside cannot see
The forms I see, nor hear the sounds I hear;
He but perceives what is; while unto me
All that has been is visible and clear.

We have no title-deeds to house or lands;
Owners and occupants of earlier dates
From graves forgotten stretch their dusty hands,
And hold in mortmain still their old estates.

The spirit-world around this world of sense
Floats like an atmosphere, and everywhere
Wafts through these earthly mists and vapours dense
A vital breath of more ethereal air.

Our little lives are kept in equipoise
By opposite attractions and desires;
The struggle of the instinct that enjoys,
And the more noble instinct that aspires.

These perturbations, this perpetual jar
Of earthly wants and aspirations high,
Come from the influence of an unseen star
An undiscovered planet in our sky.

And as the moon from some dark gate of cloud
Throws o'er the sea a floating bridge of light,
Across whose trembling planks our fancies crowd
Into the realm of mystery and night,—

So from the world of spirits there descends
A bridge of light, connecting it with this,
O'er whose unsteady floor, that sways and bends,
Wander our thoughts above the dark abyss.

SYNOPSIS

Henry Wadsworth Longfellow's "Haunted Houses," describes the ethereal imprints of those who lived in our homes before us.

ENRICHMENT ACTIVITIES

1. **Recite Poem Information**
   Recite the title of the poem, the name of the poet, and the poem.

2. **Study the Poem Pictures**
   Study the poem pictures, and describe how they relate to the poem.

3. **Describe the Setting**
   Describe aloud the scene described in the following lines of the poem.

   And as the moon from some dark gate of cloud
   Throws o'er the sea a floating bridge of light,
   Across whose trembling planks our fancies crowd

VOCABULARY (Students copy definitions from the mini dictionary at the end of the book.)

Recite and Copy Each Word	Write the Definition
wherein	
haunted	
phantoms	
errands	
glide	
impalpable	
impressions	

Recite and Copy Each Word	Write the Definition
to and fro	
illuminated	
thronged	
inoffensive	
perceives	
unto	
title-deeds	
mortmain	
estates	
atmosphere	
wafts	
vapours (vapors)	

Recite and Copy Each Word	Write the Definition
dense	
vital	
ethereal	
equipoise	
aspires / aspirations	
perturbations	
perpetual	
jar	
planks	
fancies	
realm	
abyss	

NARRATE THE POEM (Students write a summary of the poem in their own words.)

_____

_____

_____

_____

_____

_____

COPY THE EXCERPT (Students copy the provided poem excerpt.)

There are more guests at table than the hosts
Invited; the illuminated hall
Is thronged with quiet, inoffensive ghosts

_____

_____

_____

_____

NARRATE THE EXCERPT (Students write a summary of the excerpt in their own words.)

DICTATE THE EXCERPT (Instructors recite the excerpt, and students write the words.)

DRAW THE POEM (Students create a visual representation of the poem.)

Poem Title:	Poem Author:

LESSON 10. "PAUL REVERE'S RIDE" BY HENRY WADSWORTH LONGFELLOW

FEATURED POEM

Listen, my children, and you shall hear
Of the midnight ride of Paul Revere,
On the eighteenth of April, in Seventy-Five:
Hardly a man is now alive
Who remembers that famous day and year.

He said to his friend, "If the British march
By land or sea from the town tonight,
Hang a lantern aloft in the belfry-arch
Of the North-Church-tower, as a signal-light,--
One if by land, and two if by sea;
And I on the opposite shore will be,
Ready to ride and spread the alarm
Through every Middlesex village and farm,
For the country-folk to be up and to arm."

Then he said "Good night!" and with muffled oar
Silently rowed to the Charlestown shore,
Just as the moon rose over the bay,
Where swinging wide at her moorings lay
The Somerset, British man-of-war:
A phantom ship, with each mast and spar
Across the moon, like a prison-bar,
And a huge black hulk, that was magnified
By its own reflection in the tide.

Meanwhile, his friend, through alley and street
Wanders and watches with eager ears,
Till in the silence around him he hears
The muster of men at the barrack door,
The sound of arms, and the tramp of feet,
And the measured tread of the grenadiers
Marching down to their boats on the shore.

Then he climbed the tower of the old North Church,
Up the wooden stairs, with stealthy tread,
To the belfry-chamber overhead,
And startled the pigeons from their perch
On the sombre rafters, that round him made
Masses and moving shapes of shade,--
By the trembling ladder, steep and tall,
To the highest window in the wall,
Where he paused to listen and look down
A moment on the roofs of the town,
And the moonlight flowing over all.

Beneath, in the churchyard, lay the dead,
In their night-encampment on the hill,
Wrapped in silence so deep and still
That he could hear, like a sentinel's tread,
The watchful night-wind, as it went
Creeping along from tent to tent,
And seeming to whisper, "All is well!"
A moment only he feels the spell
Of the place and the hour, and the secret dread
Of the lonely belfry and the dead;
For suddenly all his thoughts are bent
On a shadowy something far away,
Where the river widens to meet the bay, --
A line of black, that bends and floats
On the rising tide, like a bridge of boats.

Meanwhile, impatient to mount and ride,
Booted and spurred, with a heavy stride,
On the opposite shore walked Paul Revere.
Now he patted his horse's side,
Now he gazed on the landscape far and near,
Then impetuous stamped the earth,
And turned and tightened his saddle-girth;
But mostly he watched with eager search
The belfry-tower of the old North Church,
As it rose above the graves on the hill,
Lonely and spectral and sombre and still.
And lo! as he looks, on the belfry's height,
A glimmer, and then a gleam of light!
He springs to the saddle, the bridle he turns,
But lingers and gazes, till full on his sight
A second lamp in the belfry burns!

A hurry of hoofs in a village-street,
A shape in the moonlight, a bulk in the dark,
And beneath from the pebbles, in passing, a spark
Struck out by a steed flying fearless and fleet:
That was all! And yet, through the gloom and the light,
The fate of a nation was riding that night;
And the spark struck out by that steed, in his flight,
Kindled the land into flame with its heat.

He has left the village and mounted the steep,
And beneath him, tranquil and broad and deep,
Is the Mystic, meeting the ocean tides;
And under the alders, that skirt its edge,
Now soft on the sand, now loud on the ledge,
Is heard the tramp of his steed as he rides.

It was twelve by the village clock
When he crossed the bridge into Medford town.
He heard the crowing of the cock,
And the barking of the farmer's dog,
And felt the damp of the river-fog,
That rises after the sun goes down.

It was one by the village clock,
When he galloped into Lexington.
He saw the gilded weathercock
Swim in the moonlight as he passed,
And the meeting-house windows, blank and bare,
Gaze at him with a spectral glare,
As if they already stood aghast
At the bloody work they would look upon.

It was two by the village clock,

When he came to the bridge in Concord town.

He heard the bleating of the flock,

And the twitter of birds among the trees,

And felt the breath of the morning breeze

Blowing over the meadows brown.

And one was safe and asleep in his bed

Who at the bridge would be first to fall,

Who that day would be lying dead,

Pierced by a British musket-ball.

You know the rest. In the books you have read,

How the British Regulars fired and fled,--

How the farmers gave them ball for ball,

From behind each fence and farmyard-wall,

Chasing the red-coats down the lane,

Then crossing the fields to emerge again

Under the trees at the turn of the road,

And only pausing to fire and load.

So through the night rode Paul Revere;

And so through the night went his cry of alarm

To every Middlesex village and farm,--

A cry of defiance, and not of fear,

A voice in the darkness, a knock at the door,

And a word that shall echo forevermore!

For, borne on the night-wind of the Past,

Through all our history, to the last,

In the hour of darkness and peril and need,

The people will waken and listen to hear

The hurrying hoof-beats of that steed,

And the midnight message of Paul Revere.

SYNOPSIS

Henry Wadsworth Longfellow's "Paul Revere's Ride" describes a Revolutionary War event that Longfellow rearranged and dramatized to create a more compelling story. In the poem, Paul Revere awaits a signal indicating the British are attacking Middlesex County, Massachusetts. Revere's friend is to hang one lantern from the church tower if the British are marching by land and two lanterns if the British are invading by sea. When two lanterns burn from the belfry, Paul Revere rides throughout the night to call his compatriots to arms in preparation for an attack from the sea.

ENRICHMENT ACTIVITIES

1. **Recite Poem Information**
   Recite the title of the poem, the name of the poet, and the poem.

2. **Study the Poem Pictures**
   Study the poem pictures, and describe how they relate to the poem.

3. **Map the Poem**
   - In the poem, Paul Revere rides to every Middlesex village and farm.
   - Middlesex county is in Massachusetts. Color Massachusetts (MA) on the map of the United States.

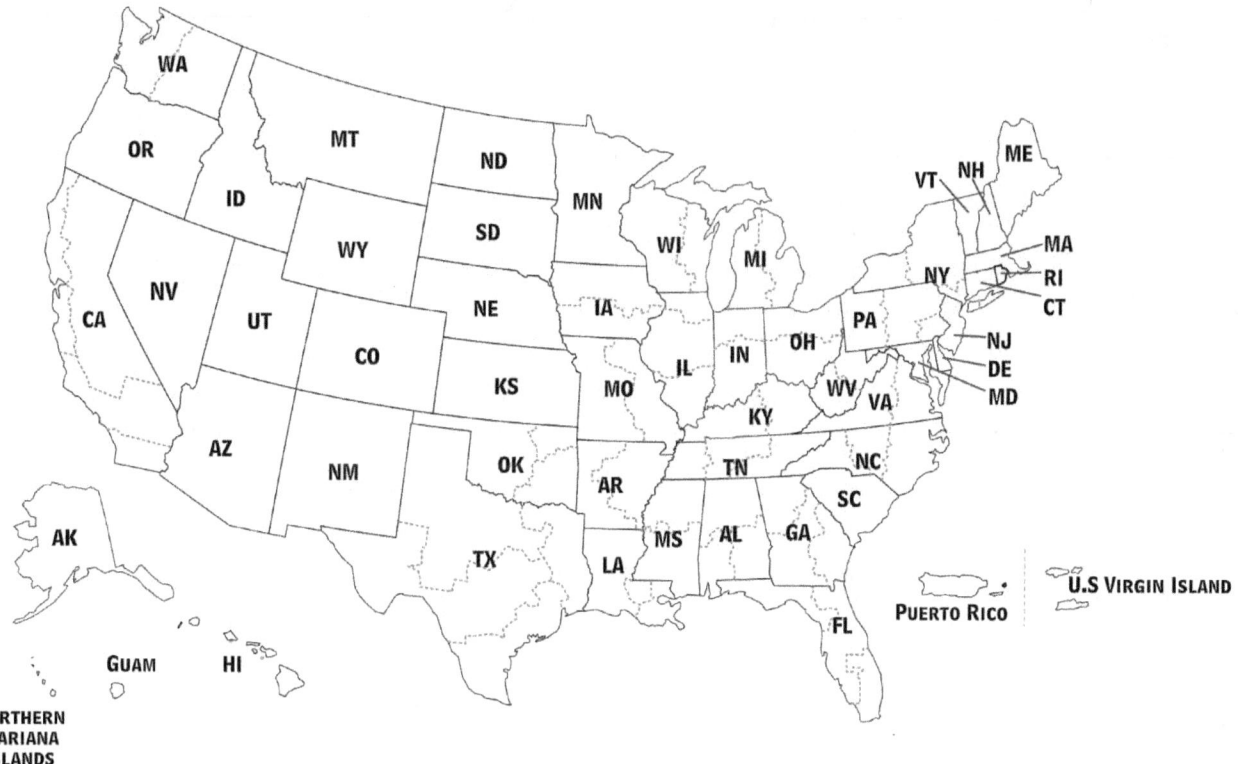

VOCABULARY (Students copy definitions from the mini dictionary at the end of the book.)

Recite and Copy Each Word	Write the Definition
aloft	
belfry	
signal	
muffled	
bay	
moorings	
spar	
magnified	
muster	
barrack	
arms	
grenadiers	

Recite and Copy Each Word	Write the Definition
tower	
stealthy	
sombre (somber)	
encampment	
sentinel	
impatient	
impetuous	
girth	
spectral	
bridle	
steed	
fleet	

Recite and Copy Each Word	Write the Definition
kindled	
tranquil	
mystic	
alders	
gilded	
weathercock	
aghast	
defiance	
forevermore	
peril	

NARRATE THE POEM (Students write a summary of the poem in their own words.)

COPY THE EXCERPT (Students copy the provided poem excerpt.)

One if by land, and two if by sea;
And I on the opposite shore will be,
Ready to ride and spread the alarm
Through every Middlesex village and farm

NARRATE THE EXCERPT (Students write a summary of the excerpt in their own words.)

DICTATE THE EXCERPT (Instructors recite the excerpt, and students write the words.)

DRAW THE POEM (Students create a visual representation of the poem.)

Poem Title:	Poem Author:

LESSON 11. "THE TIDE RISES, THE TIDE FALLS" BY HENRY WADSWORTH LONGFELLOW

FEATURED POEM

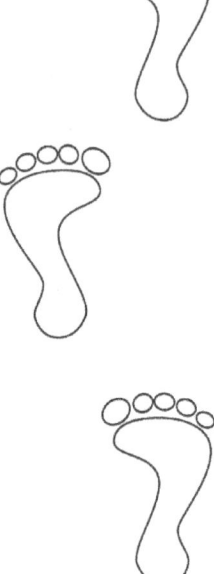

The tide rises, the tide falls,
The twilight darkens, the curlew calls;
Along the sea-sands damp and brown
The traveler hastens toward the town,
And the tide rises, the tide falls.

Darkness settles on roofs and walls,
But the sea, the sea in the darkness calls;
The little waves, with their soft, white hands,
Efface the footprints in the sands,
And the tide rises, the tide falls.

The morning breaks; the steeds in their stalls
Stamp and neigh, as the hostler calls;
The day returns, but nevermore
Returns the traveler to the shore,
And the tide rises, the tide falls.

SYNOPSIS

Henry Wadsworth Longfellow's poem, "The Tide Rises, the Tide Falls," describes the never-ending rise and fall of the ocean as people go about their daily business. The business of people matters not to the sea. No matter what people do, the tide rises, the tide falls.

ENRICHMENT ACTIVITIES

1. **Recite Poem Information**
   Recite the title of the poem, the name of the poet, and the poem.

2. **Study the Poem Pictures**
   Study the poem pictures, and describe how they relate to the poem.

3. **Discuss Tide Pools**
   - When the ocean tide falls, it may leave behind tide pools, shallow pools of seawater cradled in depressions in the rocks.
   - Animals such as starfish, mussels, clams, sea anemones, chitons, crabs, and green algae live in tide pools.
   - Draw some animals in the tide pool below.

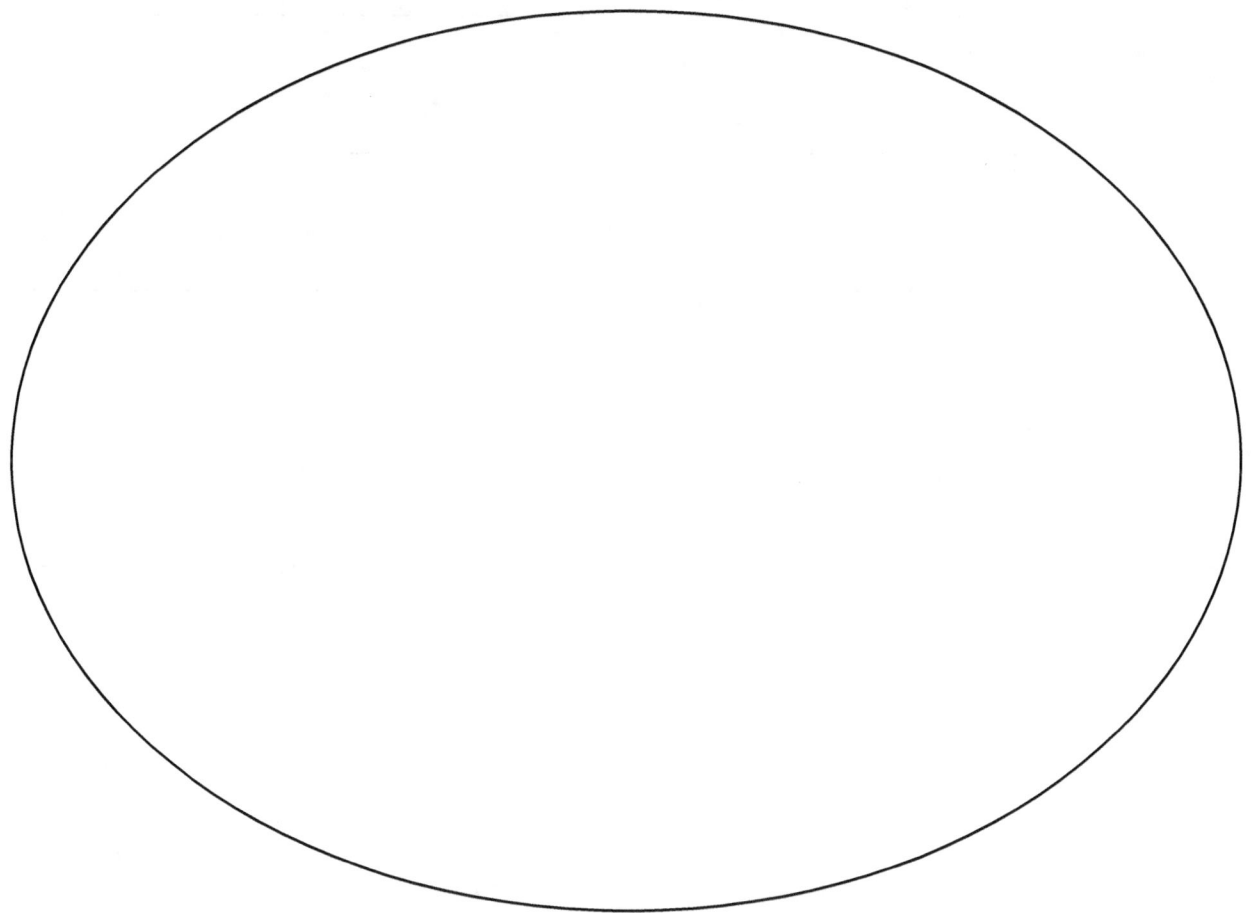

VOCABULARY (Students copy definitions from the mini dictionary at the end of the book.)

Recite and Copy Each Word	Write the Definition
tide	
rises	
twilight	
curlew	
hastens	
settles	
efface	
steeds	
hostler	
nevermore	

NARRATE THE POEM (Students write a summary of the poem in their own words.)

_____

_____

_____

_____

_____

_____

COPY THE EXCERPT (Students copy the provided poem excerpt.)

The little waves, with their soft, white hands,
Efface the footprints in the sands,
And the tide rises, the tide falls.

_____

_____

_____

_____

_____

NARRATE THE EXCERPT (Students write a summary of the excerpt in their own words.)

DICTATE THE EXCERPT (Instructors recite the excerpt, and students write the words.)

DRAW THE POEM (Students create a visual representation of the poem.)

Poem Title:	Poem Author:

LESSON 12. "SNOW-FLAKES"
BY HENRY WADSWORTH LONGFELLOW

FEATURED POEM

Out of the bosom of the Air,
Out of the cloud-folds of her garments shaken,
Over the woodlands brown and bare,
Over the harvest-fields forsaken,
Silent, and soft, and slow
Descends the snow.

Even as our cloudy fancies take
Suddenly shape in some divine expression,
Even as the troubled heart doth make
In the white countenance confession,
The troubled sky reveals
The grief it feels.

This is the poem of the air,
Slowly in silent syllables recorded;
This is the secret of despair,
Long in its cloudy bosom hoarded,
Now whispered and revealed
To wood and field.

SYNOPSIS

The first stanza of Henry Wadsworth Longfellow's "Snow-flakes," depicts the sky as a lady shaking snowflakes from the folds of her gown of clouds. The second and third stanzas describe how the snowflakes blanket the earth below with sadness.

ENRICHMENT ACTIVITIES

1. **Recite Poem Information**
   Recite the title of the poem, the name of the poet, and the poem.

2. **Study the Poem Pictures**
   Study the poem pictures, and describe how they relate to the poem.

3. **Discuss Metaphors**
   In this poem, Longfellow employs a literary device called a metaphor.
   - A metaphor uses a word or phrase to refer to something that it is not to make an implied comparison.
   - This poem describes the air/sky as a lady and the clouds as her gown.
   - Is the sky really a lady? No, but it invokes an image in the mind of the poem reader.
   - Imagine a lovely lady in the sky, wearing a gown made of clouds from which snowflakes fall.

VOCABULARY (Students copy definitions from the mini dictionary at the end of the book.)

Recite and Copy Each Word	Write the Definition
bosom	
garments	
forsaken	
descends	
fancies	
divine	
doth	
countenance	
grief	
hoarded	

NARRATE THE POEM (Students write a summary of the poem in their own words.)

COPY THE EXCERPT (Students copy the provided poem excerpt.)

Over the harvest-fields forsaken,
Silent, and soft, and slow
Descends the snow.

NARRATE THE EXCERPT (Students write a summary of the excerpt in their own words.)

DICTATE THE EXCERPT (Instructors recite the excerpt, and students write the words.)

DRAW THE POEM (Students create a visual representation of the poem.)

Poem Title:	Poem Author:

POET IV: PAUL LAURENCE DUNBAR
LESSON 13. "WE WEAR THE MASK"

POET OVERVIEW

- Paul Laurence Dunbar was born in 1872 in Dayton, Ohio.
- Dunbar's parents were slaves in Kentucky before being emancipated after the American Civil War.
- Dunbar started writing poetry as a child and published his first poem at the age of 16.
- Dunbar was editor of his high school newspaper and president of his high school literary society.
- In addition to being a poet, Dunbar was a novelist, playwright, and lyricist.
- Dunbar was the first black American poet to attain widespread international recognition.
- Dunbar died of tuberculosis in Dayton, Ohio at the age of 33.

COLOR THE POET

MAP THE POET

Locate and color Dunbar's state of birth and death, **Ohio (OH)**, on the map of the United States. Find **Kentucky (KY)**, where Dunbar's parents were slaves.

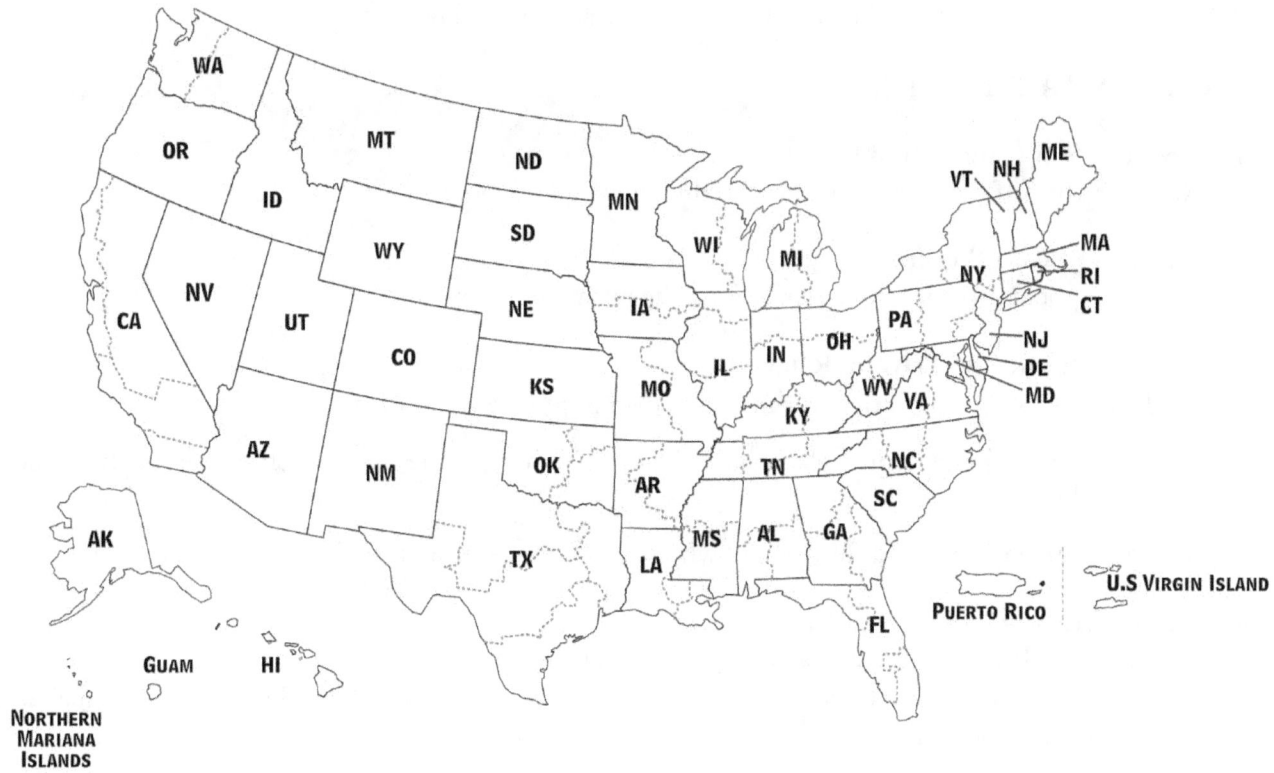

FEATURED POEM

We wear the mask that grins and lies,
It hides our cheeks and shades our eyes,—
This debt we pay to human guile;
With torn and bleeding hearts we smile
And mouth with myriad subtleties,

Why should the world be over-wise,
In counting all our tears and sighs?
Nay, let them only see us, while
We wear the mask.

We smile, but oh great Christ, our cries
To thee from tortured souls arise.
We sing, but oh the clay is vile
Beneath our feet, and long the mile,
But let the world dream otherwise,
We wear the mask!

SYNOPSIS

Paul Laurence Dunbar's "We Wear the Mask," describes how people wear the protective mask of a public persona to hide our vulnerable true selves and feelings. According to the book, "Paul Laurence Dunbar," by Peter Revell, Dunbar wrote specifically about how black Americans in the late nineteenth century felt pressured to feign happiness to contend with racial discrimination and tensions.

ENRICHMENT ACTIVITIES

1. **Recite Poem Information**
   Recite the title of the poem, the name of the poet, and the poem.

2. **Study the Poem Pictures**
   Study the poem pictures, and describe how they relate to the poem.

3. **Discuss Public and Private Behaviors**
   - How do you behave differently in public than in private?
   - Do you ever feel like you can't be yourself around other people? If so, describe one situation where you felt this way.
   - Are there people in your life around whom you remove your "mask?" If so, who are they?

4. **Revisit Metaphors**
   In this poem, Paul Dunbar used a literary device called a metaphor.
   - Remember, a metaphor uses a word or phrase to refer to something that it is not to make an implied comparison.
   - Describe how the mask serves as a metaphor in this poem.
   - Given a mask as a metaphor, what might show through if our "masks" were to crack?

VOCABULARY (Students copy definitions from the mini dictionary at the end of the book.)

Recite and Copy Each Word	Write the Definition
grins	
lies	
shades	
guile	
myriad	
subtleties	
over-wise (overwise)	
thee	
tortured	
vile	

NARRATE THE POEM (Students write a summary of the poem in their own words.)

___

___

___

___

___

___

___

COPY THE EXCERPT (Students copy the provided poem excerpt.)

We wear the mask that grins and lies,
It hides our cheeks and shades our eyes

___

___

___

___

___

NARRATE THE EXCERPT (Students write a summary of the excerpt in their own words.)

DICTATE THE EXCERPT (Instructors recite the excerpt, and students write the words.)

DRAW THE POEM (Students create a visual representation of the poem.)

Poem Title:	Poem Author:

LESSON 14. "THE SEEDLING"
BY PAUL LAURENCE DUNBAR

FEATURED POEM

1. As a quiet little seedling
   Lay within its darksome bed,
   To itself it fell a-talking,
   And this is what it said:

2. "I am not so very robust,
   But I'll do the best I can;"
   And the seedling from that moment
   Its work of life began.

3. So it pushed a little leaflet
   Up into the light of day,
   To examine the surroundings
   And show the rest the way.

4. The leaflet liked the prospect,
   So it called its brother, Stem;
   Then two other leaflets heard it,
   And quickly followed them.

5. To be sure, the haste and hurry
   Made the seedling sweat and pant;
   But almost before it knew it
   It found itself a plant.

6. The sunshine poured upon it,
   And the clouds they gave a shower;
   And the little plant kept growing
   Till it found itself a flower.

7. Little folks, be like the seedling,
   Always do the best you can;
   Every child must share life's labor
   Just as well as every man.

8. And the sun and showers will help you
   Through the lonesome, struggling hours,
   Till you raise to light and beauty
   Virtue's fair, unfading flowers.

SYNOPSIS

Paul Laurence Dunbar's "The Seedling," describes how a tiny, powerless seedling strives to become a strong plant and a beautiful flower. Dunbar encourages every child to try their very best and conveys that persevering through both the good times and the bad will lead people to strength and beauty, just like the little seedling.

ENRICHMENT ACTIVITIES

1. **Recite Poem Information**
   Recite the title of the poem, the name of the poet, and the poem.

2. **Study the Poem Pictures**
   Study the poem pictures, and describe how they relate to the poem.

3. **Discuss Perseverance**
   Perseverance is defined as continuing in a course of action without regard to discouragement, opposition, or previous failure.
   - Have you ever felt like giving up? If so, describe the situation and the outcome. Did you give up or did you keep trying?
   - Have you ever overcome an obstacle in life? If so, describe the situation and the outcome.

4. **Revisit Metaphors**
   In this poem, Paul Dunbar used a literary device called a metaphor.
   - Remember, a metaphor uses a word or phrase to refer to something that it is not to make an implied comparison.
   - Describe how the seedling serves as a metaphor in this poem.
   - Given a seedling as a metaphor, what might serve as fertilizer for the "seedling?"

VOCABULARY (Students copy definitions from the mini dictionary at the end of the book.)

Recite and Copy Each Word	Write the Definition
seedling	
darksome	
robust	
leaflet	
examine	
surroundings	
prospect	
haste	
labor	
virtue	

NARRATE THE POEM (Students write a summary of the poem in their own words.)

___

___

___

___

___

___

COPY THE EXCERPT (Students copy the provided poem excerpt.)

Little folks, be like the seedling,
Always do the best you can

___

___

___

___

NARRATE THE EXCERPT (Students write a summary of the excerpt in their own words.)

DICTATE THE EXCERPT (Instructors recite the excerpt, and students write the words.)

DRAW THE POEM (Students create a visual representation of the poem.)

Poem Title:	Poem Author:

LESSON 15. "SUNSET"
BY PAUL LAURENCE DUNBAR

FEATURED POEM

The river sleeps beneath the sky,

And clasps the shadows to its breast;

The crescent moon shines dim on high;

And in the lately radiant west

The gold is fading into gray.

Now stills the lark his festive lay,

And mourns with me the dying day.

While in the south the first faint star

Lifts to the night its silver face,

And twinkles to the moon afar

Across the heaven's graying space,

Low murmurs reach me from the town,

As Day puts on her sombre crown,

And shakes her mantle darkly down.

SYNOPSIS

Paul Laurence Dunbar's "Sunset," describes the sights, sounds, and activities surrounding the fall of day and the rise of night.

ENRICHMENT ACTIVITIES

1. **Recite Poem Information**
   Recite the title of the poem, the name of the poet, and the poem.

2. **Study the Poem Pictures**
   Study the poem pictures, and describe how they relate to the poem.

3. **Describe a Beautiful Sunset**
   Have you ever seen a beautiful sunset? If you haven't, on a clear day observe the sun as it disappears.
   - Describe the colors in the sky.
   - Describe the quality of light.
   - Describe how the beautiful sunset made you feel.

4. **Revisit Metaphors**
   In this poem, Paul Dunbar uses a literary device called a metaphor.
   - Remember, a metaphor uses a word or phrase to refer to something that it is not to make an implied comparison.
   - Identify the lines in the poem where Dunbar uses a queen as a metaphor for the day.

VOCABULARY (Students copy definitions from the mini dictionary at the end of the book.)

Recite and Copy Each Word	Write the Definition
clasps	
crescent	
radiant	
lark	
festive	
lay	
mourns	
murmurs	
sombre (somber)	
mantle	

NARRATE THE POEM (Students write a summary of the poem in their own words.)

_____

_____

_____

_____

_____

COPY THE EXCERPT (Students copy the provided poem excerpt.)

And in the lately radiant west
The gold is fading into gray.

_____

_____

_____

_____

NARRATE THE EXCERPT (Students write a summary of the excerpt in their own words.)

DICTATE THE EXCERPT (Instructors recite the excerpt, and students write the words.)

DRAW THE POEM (Students create a visual representation of the poem.)

Poem Title:	Poem Author:

LESSON 16. "HE HAD HIS DREAM" BY PAUL LAURENCE DUNBAR

FEATURED POEM

He had his dream, and all through life,
Worked up to it through toil and strife.
Afloat fore'er before his eyes,
It colored for him all his skies:

The storm–cloud dark
Above his bark,
The calm and listless vault of blue
Took on its hopeful hue,

It tinctured every passing beam—
He had his dream.
He labored hard and failed at last,
His sails too weak to bear the blast,

The raging tempests tore away
And sent his beating bark astray.
But what cared he
For wind or sea!

He said, "The tempest will be short,
My bark will come to port."
He saw through every cloud a gleam—
He had his dream.

SYNOPSIS

Paul Laurence Dunbar's "He Had His Dream," describes a man who works his whole life toward a dream. The man hasn't achieved his dream by the end of the poem, but he doesn't give up. He continues to toil and strive.

ENRICHMENT ACTIVITIES

1. **Recite Poem Information**
   Recite the title of the poem, the name of the poet, and the poem.

2. **Study the Poem Pictures**
   Study the poem pictures, and describe how they relate to the poem.

3. **Discuss Your Dreams**
   - What are your dreams for life?
   - What obstacles might keep you from accomplishing your dreams?
   - Do you have a plan for achieving your dreams? If so, what is it?

4. **Revisit Metaphors**
   In this poem, Paul Dunbar used a literary device called a metaphor.
   - Remember, a metaphor uses a word or phrase to refer to something that it is not to make an implied comparison.
   - Identify the lines of the poem where a ship is used as a metaphor.
   - Describe how the ship serves as a metaphor in this poem.

VOCABULARY (Students copy definitions from the mini dictionary at the end of the book.)

Recite and Copy Each Word	Write the Definition
dream	
toil	
strife	
bark	

Recite and Copy Each Word	Write the Definition
listless	
vault	
hue	
tinctured	
labored	
tempests	
astray	
port	
gleam	

NARRATE THE POEM (Students write a summary of the poem in their own words.)

COPY THE EXCERPT (Students copy the provided poem excerpt.)

He had his dream, and all through life,
Worked up to it through toil and strife.

NARRATE THE EXCERPT (Students write a summary of the excerpt in their own words.)

DICTATE THE EXCERPT (Instructors recite the excerpt, and students write the words.)

DRAW THE POEM (Students create a visual representation of the poem.)

Poem Title:	Poem Author:

ELEMENTARY POETRY VOLUME 4: ADVANCING IN POETRY

POET V: CHRISTINA GEORGINA ROSSETTI
LESSON 17. "A BIRTHDAY"

POET OVERVIEW

- Christina Georgina Rossetti was born in 1830 in London, England (United Kingdom).
- Rossetti had an artistic family. Her father was a poet and a teacher, one of her siblings was an artist and a poet, and her other two siblings were writers.
- Rossetti was homeschooled by her parents and studied religious books, works of fiction, and fairy tales.
- Rossetti published her first poems when she was 18 and a full volume of poetry at age 31.
- Rossetti died of cancer in London, England at the age of 64.

COLOR THE POET

MAP THE POET

Locate and color Rossetti's country of birth, **England (United Kingdom)**, on the map of Europe. Circle **London**, her city of birth.

FEATURED POEM

My heart is like a singing bird
Whose nest is in a water'd shoot;
My heart is like an apple-tree
Whose boughs are bent with thickset fruit;
My heart is like a rainbow shell
That paddles in a halcyon sea;
My heart is gladder than all these
Because my love is come to me.

Raise me a dais of silk and down;
Hang it with vair and purple dyes;
Carve it in doves and pomegranates,
And peacocks with a hundred eyes;
Work it in gold and silver grapes,
In leaves and silver fleurs-de-lys;
Because the birthday of my life
Is come, my love is come to me.

SYNOPSIS

Christina Georgina Rossetti's "A Birthday," uses similes to describe the happiness of the narrator upon being united with their true love. This poem doesn't celebrate a traditional birthday of a baby being born. Instead, the narrator celebrates the birthday of their new life, which has begun upon being reunited with their love.

ENRICHMENT ACTIVITIES

1. **Recite Poem Information**
   Recite the title of the poem, the name of the poet, and the poem.

2. **Study the Poem Pictures**
   Study the poem pictures, and describe how they relate to the poem.

3. **Discuss Your Birthday**
   - When is your birthday?
   - What happened on your original birthday?
   - If you could do anything on your next birthday, what would you do?

4. **Discuss Similes**
   - In this poem, Christina Rossetti uses a literary device called a simile.
   - A simile is figure of speech in which one thing is compared to another, in the case of English generally using **like** or **as**.
   - Examples of similes from the poem include the following:
     o My heart is **like** a singing bird
     o My heart is **like** an apple-tree.
   - Find an additional simile in the poem.

VOCABULARY (Students copy definitions from the mini dictionary at the end of the book.)

Recite and Copy Each Word	Write the Definition
shoot	
boughs	
thickset	
halcyon	
dais	
silk	
down	
vair	
pomegranates	
fleurs-de-lys	

NARRATE THE POEM (Students write a summary of the poem in their own words.)

COPY THE EXCERPT (Students copy the provided poem excerpt.)

Because the birthday of my life
Is come, my love is come to me.

NARRATE THE EXCERPT (Students write a summary of the excerpt in their own words.)

DICTATE THE EXCERPT (Instructors recite the excerpt, and students write the words.)

DRAW THE POEM (Students create a visual representation of the poem.)

Poem Title:	Poem Author:

ELEMENTARY POETRY VOLUME 4: ADVANCING IN POETRY

LESSON 18. "UPHILL"
BY CHRISTINA GEORGINA ROSSETTI

FEATURED POEM

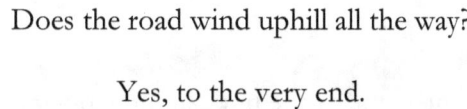

Does the road wind uphill all the way?

Yes, to the very end.

Will the day's journey take the whole long day?

From morn to night, my friend.

But is there for the night a resting-place?

A roof for when the slow dark hours begin.

May not the darkness hide it from my face?

You cannot miss that inn.

Shall I meet other wayfarers at night?

Those who have gone before.

Then must I knock, or call when just in sight?

They will not keep you standing at that door.

Shall I find comfort, travel-sore and weak?

Of labour you shall find the sum.

Will there be beds for me and all who seek?

Yea, beds for all who come.

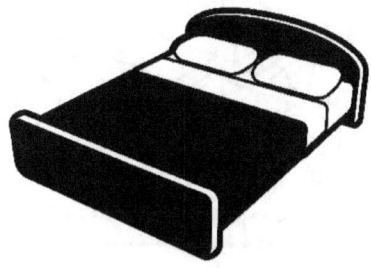

SYNOPSIS

Christina Georgina Rossetti's "Uphill," employs a journey up a winding road as a metaphor for life. The poem features two people conversing, one asking questions and another answering the questions. The journey culminates at an inn, where there are beds for all who arrive.

ENRICHMENT ACTIVITIES

1. **Recite Poem Information**
   Recite the title of the poem, the name of the poet, and the poem.

2. **Study the Poem Pictures**
   Study the poem pictures, and describe how they relate to the poem.

3. **Revisit Metaphors**
   In this poem, Christina Rossetti used a literary device called a metaphor.
   - Remember, a metaphor uses a word or phrase to refer to something that it is not to make an implied comparison.
   - Identify the lines of the poem where a road is used as a metaphor.
   - Describe how the road serves as a metaphor in this poem.

4. **Discuss the Poem**
   - Why would Rossetti describe life as uphill and winding?
   - Why can't we miss the inn in the poem?
   - Who do you think are the other wayfarers who have gone before us?
   - Why won't the inn ever run out of beds?

VOCABULARY (Students copy definitions from the mini dictionary at the end of the book.)

Recite and Copy Each Word	Write the Definition
wind	
uphill	
morn	
inn	
wayfarers	
comfort	
labour (labor)	
sum	
seek	
yea	

NARRATE THE POEM (Students write a summary of the poem in their own words.)

COPY THE EXCERPT (Students copy the provided poem excerpt.)

May not the darkness hide it from my face?
You cannot miss that inn.

NARRATE THE EXCERPT (Students write a summary of the excerpt in their own words.)

DICTATE THE EXCERPT (Instructors recite the excerpt, and students write the words.)

DRAW THE POEM (Students create a visual representation of the poem.)

Poem Title:	Poem Author:

ELEMENTARY POETRY VOLUME 4: ADVANCING IN POETRY

LESSON 19. "THE QUEEN OF HEARTS" BY CHRISTINA GEORGINA ROSSETTI

FEATURED POEM

How comes it, Flora, that, whenever we
Play cards together, you invariably,
However the pack parts,
Still hold the Queen of Hearts?

I've scanned you with a scrutinizing gaze,
Resolved to fathom these your secret ways:
But, sift them as I will,
Your ways are secret still.

I cut and shuffle; shuffle, cut, again;
But all my cutting, shuffling, proves in vain:
Vain hope, vain forethought, too;
That Queen still falls to you.

I dropped her once, prepense; but, ere the deal
Was dealt, your instinct seemed her loss to feel:
"There should be one card more,"
You said, and searched the floor.

I cheated once: I made a private notch
In Heart-Queen's back, and kept a lynx-eyed watch;
Yet such another back
Deceived me in the pack:

The Queen of Clubs assumed by arts unknown
An imitative dint that seemed my own;
This notch, not of my doing,
Misled me to my ruin.

It baffles me to puzzle out the clew,
Which must be skill, or craft, or luck in you:
Unless, indeed, it be
Natural affinity.

SYNOPSIS

In Christina Georgina Rossetti's "The Queen of Hearts," the narrator describes that how no matter what she does, her competitor, Flora, always comes up with the Queen of Hearts. Even when the narrator cheats, Flora still wins the Queen of Hearts. Flora's constant victories continue to puzzle the narrator at the end of the poem.

ENRICHMENT ACTIVITIES

1. **Recite Poem Information**
   Recite the title of the poem, the name of the poet, and the poem.

2. **Study the Poem Pictures**
   Study the poem pictures, and describe how they relate to the poem.

3. **Discuss Cheating**
   - In the poem, the narrator attempts to cheat, but still loses.
   - Have you ever cheated? If so, describe the situation.
   - Do you think a victory won through cheating is valid?
   - Describe one way you might win without cheating.

4. **Revisit Metaphors**
   - In this poem, Christina Rossetti uses a literary device called a metaphor.
   - Remember, a metaphor uses a word or phrase to refer to something that it is not to make an implied comparison.
   - The metaphors in this poem are the game of cards and the Queen of Hearts (hint - there's a saying that some people always hold the winning card in life).
     o What do you think the game of cards represents?
     o What do you think the Queen of Hearts represents?
     o What do you think the Queen of Clubs represents?

VOCABULARY (Students copy definitions from the mini dictionary at the end of the book.)

Recite and Copy Each Word	Write the Definition
invariably	
scanned	
scrutinizing	
resolved	
fathom	
sift	
cut	
shuffle	
vain	
forethought	
prepense	
ere	

Recite and Copy Each Word	Write the Definition
notch	
lynx	
imitative	
dint	
misled	
baffles	
clew (clue)	
affinity	

NARRATE THE POEM (Students write a summary of the poem in their own words.)

COPY THE EXCERPT (Students copy the provided poem excerpt.)

Yet such another back
Deceived me in the pack

NARRATE THE EXCERPT (Students write a summary of the excerpt in their own words.)

DICTATE THE EXCERPT (Instructors recite the excerpt, and students write the words.)

DRAW THE POEM (Students create a visual representation of the poem.)

Poem Title:	Poem Author:

SONJA GLUMICH

LESSON 20. "SUMMER"
BY CHRISTINA GEORGINA ROSSETTI

FEATURED POEM

Winter is cold-hearted,
Spring is yea and nay,
Autumn is a weathercock
Blown every way:
Summer days for me
When every leaf is on its tree;

When Robin's not a beggar,
And Jenny Wren's a bride,
And larks hang singing, singing, singing,
Over the wheat-fields wide,
And anchored lilies ride,
And the pendulum spider
Swings from side to side,

And blue-black beetles transact business,
And gnats fly in a host,
And furry caterpillars hasten
That no time be lost,
And moths grow fat and thrive,
And ladybirds arrive.

Before green apples blush,
Before green nuts embrown,
Why, one day in the country
Is worth a month in town;
Is worth a day and a year
Of the dusty, musty, lag-last fashion
That days drone elsewhere.

SYNOPSIS

In Christina Georgina Rossetti's "Summer," the narrator discusses why they prefer summer over winter, spring, and autumn. The narrator also describes the plants and animals of summer and the superiority of the country over town.

ENRICHMENT ACTIVITIES

1. **Recite Poem Information**
   Recite the title of the poem, the name of the poet, and the poem.

2. **Study the Poem Pictures**
   Study the poem pictures, and describe how they relate to the poem.

3. **Discuss the Seasons**
   - Which is your favorite season?
   - Describe what you like about your favorite season.
   - Describe what you don't like about the other seasons.

4. **Find Animals and Plants**
   - Find the animals and plants mentioned in the poem.
   - How many animals are mentioned?
   - How many plants are mentioned?

VOCABULARY (Students copy definitions from the mini dictionary at the end of the book.)

Recite and Copy Each Word	Write the Definition
yea	
nay	
weathercock	
larks	
anchored	

Recite and Copy Each Word	Write the Definition
lilies	
pendulum	
transact	
host	
hasten	
thrive	
blush	
embrown	
dusty	
musty	
lag-last	
drone	

NARRATE THE POEM (Students write a summary of the poem in their own words.)

COPY THE EXCERPT (Students copy the provided poem excerpt.)

When Robin's not a beggar,
And Jenny Wren's a bride

NARRATE THE EXCERPT (Students write a summary of the excerpt in their own words.)

_____

_____

_____

_____

_____

_____

_____

DICTATE THE EXCERPT (Instructors recite the excerpt, and students write the words.)

_____

_____

_____

_____

_____

DRAW THE POEM (Students create a visual representation of the poem.)

Poem Title:	Poem Author:

POET VI: AMY LOWELL
LESSON 21. "THE TRAVELLING BEAR"

POET OVERVIEW

- Amy Lowell was born in 1874 in Brookline, Massachusetts.
- Lowell was part of an accomplished family. One of her brothers was an astronomer and the other was the president of Harvard University.
- Growing up, Lowell had a difficult time in school and was a social misfit.
- Lowell's family didn't believe women should attend college, so she was not college educated.
- Despite her educational barriers, Lowell's poems won her the Pulitzer Prize for Poetry after her death.
- Lowell died of a cerebral hemorrhage in Brookline, Massachusetts at the age of 51.

COLOR THE POET

ELEMENTARY POETRY VOLUME 4: ADVANCING IN POETRY

MAP THE POET

Locate and color Lowell's state of birth, **Massachusetts (MA),** on the map of the United States.

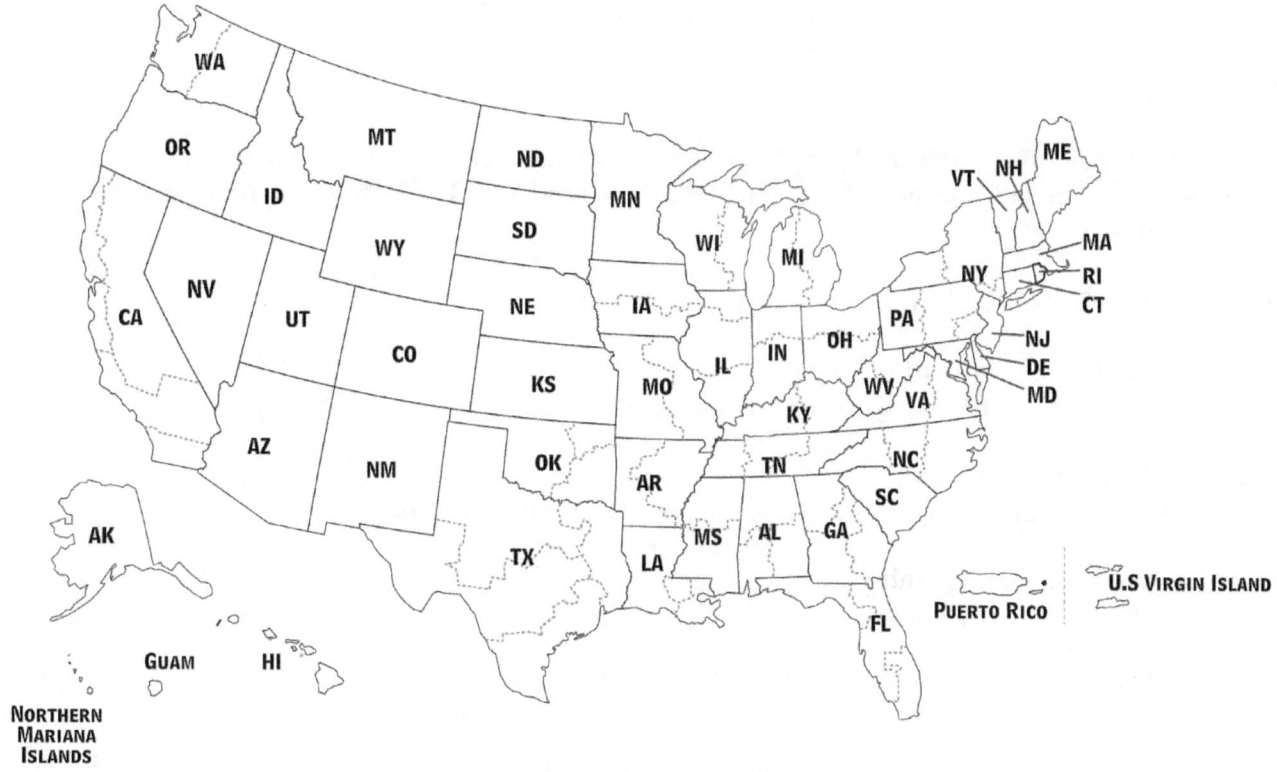

FEATURED POEM

Grass-blades push up between the cobblestones
And catch the sun on their flat sides
Shooting it back,
Gold and emerald,
Into the eyes of passers-by.

And over the cobblestones,
Square-footed and heavy,
Dances the trained bear.
The cobbles cut his feet,
And he has a ring in his nose
But still he dances,
For the keeper pricks him with a sharp stick,
Under his fur.

Now the crowd gapes and chuckles,
And boys and young women shuffle their feet in time to the dancing bear.
They see him wobbling
Against a dust of emerald and gold,
And they are greatly delighted.

The legs of the bear shake with fatigue
And his back aches,
And the shining grass-blades dazzle and confuse him.
But still he dances,
Because of the little, pointed stick.

SYNOPSIS

In Amy Lowell's "The Travelling Bear," she invites the reader to empathize with a performing bear. To the poem spectators, the performance of the bear is delightful and fun. To the bear, his performance involves only fear and pain.

ENRICHMENT ACTIVITIES

1. **Recite Poem Information**
   Recite the title of the poem, the name of the poet, and the poem.

2. **Study the Poem Pictures**
   Study the poem pictures, and describe how they relate to the poem.

3. **Discuss Performing Animals**
   - Discuss whether you think it is right for animals to perform for people, such as in circuses.

   - Discuss whether you think it is right to keep animals in a zoo. (Consider that some animals become injured and/or will not survive if released back into the wild.)

   - Discuss whether you think it is right for people to have animals as pets. Do you think it is okay to have a dog or cat as a pet? What about a wolf or a gorilla?

VOCABULARY (Students copy definitions from the mini dictionary at the end of the book.)

Recite and Copy Each Word	Write the Definition
cobblestones	
emerald	
cobbles	
pricks	
gapes	
chuckles	
wobbling	
fatigue	
aches	
dazzle	

NARRATE THE POEM (Students write a summary of the poem in their own words.)

COPY THE EXCERPT (Students copy the provided poem excerpt.)

But still he dances,
Because of the little, pointed stick.

NARRATE THE EXCERPT (Students write a summary of the excerpt in their own words.)

DICTATE THE EXCERPT (Instructors recite the excerpt, and students write the words.)

DRAW THE POEM (Students create a visual representation of the poem.)

Poem Title:	Poem Author:

LESSON 22. "TO A FRIEND"
BY AMY LOWELL

FEATURED POEM

I ask but one thing of you, only one,

That always you will be my dream of you;

That never shall I wake to find untrue

All this I have believed and rested on,

Forever vanished, like a vision gone

Out into the night. Alas, how few

There are who strike in us a chord we knew

Existed, but so seldom heard its tone

We tremble at the half-forgotten sound.

The world is full of rude awakenings

And heaven-born castles shattered to the ground,

Yet still our human longing vainly clings

To a belief in beauty through all wrongs.

O stay your hand, and leave my heart its songs!

SYNOPSIS

In Amy Lowell's "To a Friend," the narrator asks that a cherished friend remains loyal and true.

ENRICHMENT ACTIVITIES

1. **Recite Poem Information**
   Recite the title of the poem, the name of the poet, and the poem.

2. **Study the Poem Picture**
   Study the poem picture, and describe how it relates to the poem.

3. **Discuss Close Friends**
   - Discuss qualities you look for in a friend.
   - Discuss qualities you wouldn't want in a friend.
   - Has a friend ever disappointed you? Describe the situation.
   - Have you ever disappointed a friend? Describe the situation.

VOCABULARY (Students copy definitions from the mini dictionary at the end of the book.)

Recite and Copy Each Word	Write the Definition
untrue	
believed	
vanished	
vision	
alas	
strike	
chord	

Recite and Copy Each Word	Write the Definition
seldom	
tone	
tremble	
rude	
awakenings	
shattered	
longing	
vainly	
clings	
stay	

NARRATE THE POEM (Students write a summary of the poem in their own words.)

COPY THE EXCERPT (Students copy the provided poem excerpt.)

I ask but one thing of you, only one,
That always you will be my dream of you

NARRATE THE EXCERPT (Students write a summary of the excerpt in their own words.)

DICTATE THE EXCERPT (Instructors recite the excerpt, and students write the words.)

DRAW THE POEM (Students create a visual representation of the poem.)

Poem Title:	Poem Author:

ELEMENTARY POETRY VOLUME 4: ADVANCING IN POETRY

LESSON 23. "VENUS TRANSIENS"
BY AMY LOWELL

FEATURED POEM

Tell me,
Was Venus more beautiful
Than you are,
When she topped
The crinkled waves,
Drifting shoreward
On her plaited shell?

Was Botticelli's vision
Fairer than mine;
And were the painted rosebuds
He tossed his lady
Of better worth
Than the words I blow about you
To cover your too great loveliness
As with a gauze
Of misted silver?

For me,
You stand poised
In the blue and buoyant air,
Cinctured by bright winds,
Treading the sunlight.
And the waves which precede you
Ripple and stir
The sands at my feet.

SYNOPSIS

In Amy Lowell's "Venus Transiens," the narrator compares the beauty of someone she loves to the goddess Venus in Sandro Botticelli's painting, "Birth of Venus," and finds Venus lacking.

ENRICHMENT ACTIVITIES

1. **Recite Poem Information**
   Recite the title of the poem, the name of the poet, and the poem.

2. **Study the Poem Pictures**
   Study the poem pictures, and describe how they relate to the poem.

3. **Discuss Beauty**
   - The poem narrator finds the one they love very beautiful.
   - What is the most beautiful thing or person in the world to you?
   - Might it be a flower, a baby, a parent, a hug, a friend, a sunset, a pretty view, a monument, a story, a painting, a poem, a bubbling brook, a song, or the starry night sky?

VOCABULARY (Students copy definitions from the mini dictionary at the end of the book.)

Recite and Copy Each Word	Write the Definition
Venus	
crinkled	
drifting	
shoreward	
plaited	
Botticelli	
fairer	

Recite and Copy Each Word	Write the Definition
worth	
gauze	
poised	
buoyant	
cinctured	
treading	
precede	
ripple	
stir	

NARRATE THE POEM (Students write a summary of the poem in their own words.)

COPY THE EXCERPT (Students copy the provided poem excerpt.)

Was Venus more beautiful
Than you are,
When she topped
The crinkled waves

NARRATE THE EXCERPT (Students write a summary of the excerpt in their own words.)

DICTATE THE EXCERPT (Instructors recite the excerpt, and students write the words.)

DRAW THE POEM (Students create a visual representation of the poem.)

Poem Title:	Poem Author:

LESSON 24. "WINTER'S TURNING"
BY AMY LOWELL

FEATURED POEM

Snow is still on the ground,
But there is a golden brightness in the air.
Across the river,
Blue,
Blue,

Sweeping widely under the arches
Of many bridges,
Is a spire and a dome,
Clear as though ringed with ice-flakes,
Golden, and pink, and jocund.

On a near-by steeple,
A golden weather-cock flashes smartly,
His open beak "Cock-a-doodle-dooing"
Straight at the ear of Heaven.

A tall apartment house,
Crocus-coloured,
Thrusts up from the street
Like a new-sprung flower.

Another street is edged and patterned
With the bloom of bricks,
Houses and houses of rose-red bricks,
Every window a-glitter.

The city is a parterre,
Blowing and glowing,
Alight with the wind,
Washed over with gold and mercury.

Let us throw up our hats,
For we are past the age of balls
And have none handy.
Let us take hold of hands,
And race along the sidewalks,
And dodge the traffic in crowded streets.

Let us whir with the golden spoke-wheels
Of the sun.
For tomorrow Winter drops into the waste-basket,
And the calendar calls it March.

SYNOPSIS

In Amy Lowell's "Winter's Turning," she describes the signs of the end of winter spotted in a panoramic view of a city.

ENRICHMENT ACTIVITIES

1. **Recite Poem Information**
   Recite the title of the poem, the name of the poet, and the poem.

2. **Study the Poem Picture**
   Study the poem picture, and describe how it relates to the poem.

3. **Metaphor or Simile?**
   Do the following lines from the poem contain a metaphor or a simile? How do you know? Which two things are compared?

   A tall apartment house
   Thrusts up from the street
   Like a new-sprung flower

VOCABULARY (Students copy definitions from the mini dictionary at the end of the book.)

Recite and Copy Each Word	Write the Definition
sweeping	
arches	
spire	
dome	
ringed	
jocund	
steeple	

Recite and Copy Each Word	Write the Definition
weather-cock	
crocus	
thrusts	
sprung	
edged	
patterned	
parterre	
mercury	
dodge	
whir	
spoke	
wastebasket	

NARRATE THE POEM (Students write a summary of the poem in their own words.)

_____

_____

_____

_____

_____

_____

COPY THE EXCERPT (Students copy the provided poem excerpt.)

Let us throw up our hats,
For we are past the age of balls

_____

_____

_____

_____

_____

NARRATE THE EXCERPT (Students write a summary of the excerpt in their own words.)

DICTATE THE EXCERPT (Instructors recite the excerpt, and students write the words.)

DRAW THE POEM (Students create a visual representation of the poem.)

Poem Title:	Poem Author:

POET VII: JOHN KEATS
LESSON 25. "BRIGHT STAR, WOULD I WERE STEADFAST AS THOU ART"

POET OVERVIEW

- John Keats was born in 1795 in London, England (United Kingdom).
- Keats was the son of a stableman. His father cared for horses at an inn and later managed the inn.
- Keats attended boarding school starting when he was seven years old.
- By the time Keats was 16, he had lost both of his parents, his father falling from a horse and his mother dying of tuberculosis.
- Keats trained to be a doctor and received his apothecary's license, but he abandoned medicine for poetry.
- While a young man, Keats contracted tuberculosis. On the advice of his doctors, he traveled to Rome, Italy. Despite the favorable weather, he died in Italy at the age of 25.
- Keats' poetry only became popular after his death.

COLOR THE POET

MAP THE POET

Locate and color Keats' countries of birth and death, **England (United Kingdom)** and **Italy**, on the map of Europe. Circle Keats' cities of birth and death, **London** and **Rome**.

ELEMENTARY POETRY VOLUME 4: ADVANCING IN POETRY

FEATURED POEM

Bright star, would I were steadfast as thou art—
Not in lone splendor hung aloft the night
And watching, with eternal lids apart,
Like nature's patient, sleepless Eremite,

The moving waters at their priest-like task
Of pure ablution round earth's human shores,
Or gazing on the new soft-fallen mask
Of snow upon the mountains and the moors—

No—yet still steadfast, still unchangeable,
Pillow'd upon my fair love's ripening breast,
To feel forever its soft fall and swell,
Awake forever in a sweet unrest,

Still, still to hear her tender-taken breath,
And so live ever—or else swoon to death.

SYNOPSIS

John Keats wrote "Bright Star, would I were steadfast as thou art" for Fanny Brawne, his "Bright Star," to whom he formed a deep attachment. In the poem, Keats strives to remain as steady and eternal in his love as a bright star in the sky.

ENRICHMENT ACTIVITIES

1. **Recite Poem Information**
   Recite the title of the poem, the name of the poet, and the poem.

2. **Study the Poem Picture**
   Study the poem picture, and describe how it relates to the poem.

3. **Metaphor or Simile?**
   Do the following lines from the poem contain a metaphor or a simile? How do you know?

   Bright star, would I were steadfast as thou art—
   Like nature's patient, sleepless Eremite

VOCABULARY (Students copy definitions from the mini dictionary at the end of the book.)

Recite and Copy Each Word	Write the Definition
steadfast	
thou	

Recite and Copy Each Word	Write the Definition
lone	
splendor	
aloft	
eternal	
eremite	
ablution	
moors	
unchangeable	
ripening	
tender	
swoon	

NARRATE THE POEM (Students write a summary of the poem in their own words.)

___

___

___

___

___

COPY THE EXCERPT (Students copy the provided poem excerpt.)

Bright star, would I were steadfast as thou art–
And watching, with eternal lids apart

___

___

___

___

NARRATE THE EXCERPT (Students write a summary of the excerpt in their own words.)

DICTATE THE EXCERPT (Instructors recite the excerpt, and students write the words.)

DRAW THE POEM (Students create a visual representation of the poem.)

Poem Title:	Poem Author:

LESSON 26. "ODE TO AUTUMN" BY JOHN KEATS

FEATURED POEM

Season of mists and mellow fruitfulness,
Close bosom-friend of the maturing sun;
Conspiring with him how to load and bless
With fruit the vines that round the thatch-eves run;
To bend with apples the moss'd cottage-trees,
And fill all fruit with ripeness to the core;
To swell the gourd, and plump the hazel shells
With a sweet kernel; to set budding more,
And still more, later flowers for the bees,
Until they think warm days will never cease,
For Summer has over-brimmed their clammy cells.

Who hath not seen thee oft amid thy store?
Sometimes whoever seeks abroad may find
Thee sitting careless on a granary floor,
Thy hair soft-lifted by the winnowing wind;
Or on a half-reaped furrow sound asleep,
Drowsed with the fume of poppies, while thy hook
Spares the next swath and all its twined flowers:
And sometimes like a gleaner thou dost keep
Steady thy laden head across a brook;
Or by a cider-press, with patient look,
Thou watch the last oozings hours by hours.

Where are the songs of Spring? Ay, where are they?
Think not of them, thou hast thy music too,—
While barred clouds bloom the soft-dying day,
And touch the stubble-plains with rosy hue;
Then in a wailful choir the small gnats mourn
Among the river sallows, borne aloft
Or sinking as the light wind lives or dies;
And full-grown lambs loud bleat from hilly bourn;
Hedge-crickets sing; and now with treble soft
The red-breast whistles from a garden-croft;
And gathering swallows twitter in the skies.

SYNOPSIS

John Keats' "Ode to Autumn" personifies autumn and the sun as buddies working together to grow and ripen fruit and to bloom new fall flowers for the honey bees. Autumn can be found lurking everywhere, in stores of food, on granary floors, sleeping on a furrow in a field, and watching juice seep from apples in a cider press. The narrator encourages autumn to ignore the songs of spring and focus on its own special sounds, including the hum of gnats, the bleat of sheep, and the twitter of swallows gathering for their migration south.

ENRICHMENT ACTIVITIES

1. **Recite Poem Information**
   Recite the title of the poem, the name of the poet, and the poem.

2. **Study the Poem Picture**
   Study the poem picture, and describe how it relates to the poem.

3. **Revisit Personification**
   - In this poem, Keats employs a literary device called personification.
   - Personification assigns human qualities to inanimate objects or ideas.
   - Study the three poem excerpts, and explain why they serve as examples of personification:
     - (Autumn is a) Close bosom-friend of the maturing sun.
     - Thee (autumn) sitting careless on a granary floor,
     - Thy (autumn's) hair soft-lifted by the winnowing wind;

VOCABULARY (Students copy definitions from the mini dictionary at the end of the book.)

Recite and Copy Each Word	Write the Definition
ode	
mellow	
fruitfulness	
bosom-friend	
maturing	

Recite and Copy Each Word	Write the Definition
conspiring	
thatch	
eves (eaves)	
core	
gourd	
kernel	
cease	
over-brimmed	
clammy	
cells	
amid	
granary	

Recite and Copy Each Word	Write the Definition
winnowing	
reaped	
furrow	
drowsed	
poppies	
swath	
twined	
gleaner	
laden	
cider-press	
oozings	
stubble	

Recite and Copy Each Word	Write the Definition
plains	
hue	
wailful	
choir	
gnats	
mourn	
sallows	
borne	
aloft	
bourn	
treble	
croft	

NARRATE THE POEM (Students write a summary of the poem in their own words.)

COPY THE EXCERPT (Students copy the provided poem excerpt.)

Where are the songs of Spring? Ay, where are they?
Think not of them, you have your music too,—

NARRATE THE EXCERPT (Students write a summary of the excerpt in their own words.)

DICTATE THE EXCERPT (Instructors recite the excerpt, and students write the words.)

DRAW THE POEM (Students create a visual representation of the poem.)

Poem Title:	Poem Author:

LESSON 27. "ON THE GRASSHOPPER AND CRICKET" BY JOHN KEATS

FEATURED POEM

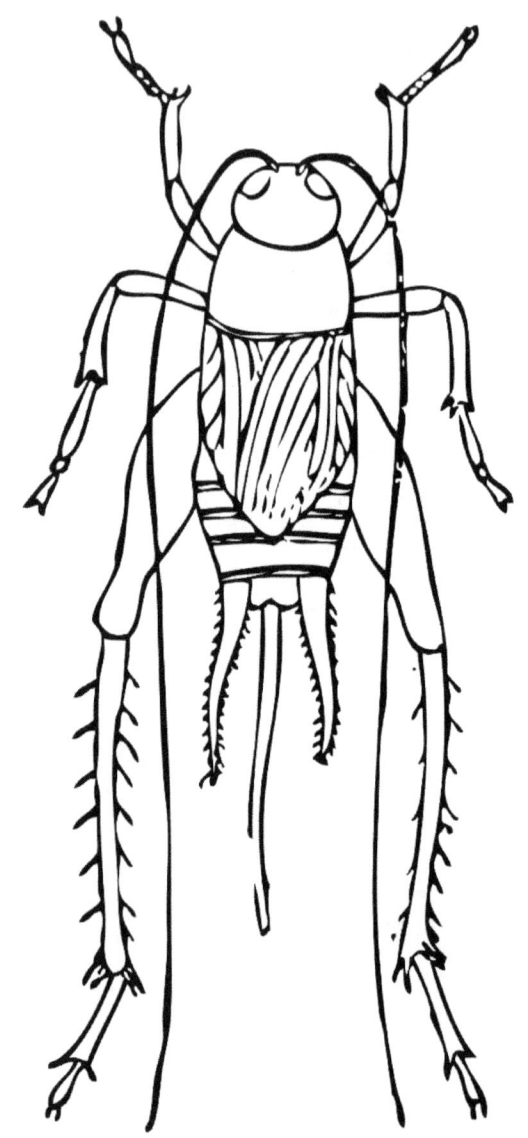

The poetry of earth is never dead:

When all the birds are faint with the hot sun,

And hide in cooling trees, a voice will run

From hedge to hedge about the new-mown mead;

That is the Grasshopper's—he takes the lead

In summer luxury,—he has never done

With his delights; for when tired out with fun

He rests at ease beneath some pleasant weed.

The poetry of earth is ceasing never:

On a lone winter evening, when the frost

Has wrought a silence, from the stove there shrills

The Cricket's song, in warmth increasing ever,

And seems to one in drowsiness half lost,

The Grasshopper's among some grassy hills.

SYNOPSIS

John Keats' "On the Grasshopper and Cricket" describes how nature still hums along despite extremes in weather. In the hottest parts of summer, the grasshopper still sings. During the coldest snaps of winter, the cricket still chirps.

ENRICHMENT ACTIVITIES

1. **Recite Poem Information**
   Recite the title of the poem, the name of the poet, and the poem.

2. **Study the Poem Picture**
   Study the poem picture, and describe how it relates to the poem.

3. **Discuss "The Poetry of Earth"**
   In the poem, Keats mentions, "the poetry of earth."
   - Explain what you think Keats means by this.
   - Describe what you especially like about "the poetry of earth."
   - For example, the fluffy clouds dotting the blue sky, the sweep of wind across lively meadows, the babbling brooks, the hum of insects, the crackle of campfires, the rustle of leaves, or the songs of birds.

VOCABULARY (Students copy definitions from the mini dictionary at the end of the book.)

Recite and Copy Each Word	Write the Definition
faint	
hedge	
mead	
luxury	
ease	
ceasing	
lone	
wrought	
shrills	

NARRATE THE POEM (Students write a summary of the poem in their own words.)

COPY THE EXCERPT (Students copy the provided poem excerpt.)

When all the birds are faint with the hot sun,
And hide in cooling trees, a voice will run

NARRATE THE EXCERPT (Students write a summary of the excerpt in their own words.)

DICTATE THE EXCERPT (Instructors recite the excerpt, and students write the words.)

DRAW THE POEM (Students create a visual representation of the poem.)

Poem Title:	Poem Author:

LESSON 28. "TO SLEEP" BY JOHN KEATS

FEATURED POEM

O soft embalmer of the still midnight,

Shutting, with careful fingers and benign,

Our gloom-pleas'd eyes, embower'd from the light,

Enshaded in forgetfulness divine:

O soothest Sleep! if so it please thee, close

In midst of this thine hymn my willing eyes,

Or wait the "Amen," ere thy poppy throws

Around my bed its lulling charities.

Then save me, or the passed day will shine

Upon my pillow, breeding many woes,—

Save me from curious Conscience, that still lords

Its strength for darkness, burrowing like a mole;

Turn the key deftly in the oiled wards,

And seal the hushed Casket of my Soul.

SYNOPSIS

John Keats' poem, "To Sleep," personifies sleep as a being who uses its fingers to close our eyes and turn the key to lock our woes within our souls.

ENRICHMENT ACTIVITIES

1. **Recite Poem Information**
   Recite the title of the poem, the name of the poet, and the poem.

2. **Study the Poem Picture**
   Study the poem picture, and describe how it relates to the poem.

3. **Revisit Personification**
   - In this poem, Keats employs a literary device called personification.
   - Personification assigns human qualities to inanimate objects or ideas.
   - Study the following poem excerpts, and explain why they provide examples of personification:
     - (Sleep) Shutting, with careful fingers and benign, Our gloom-pleas'd eyes.
     - (Sleep) Turn the key deftly in the oiled wards, And seal the hushed Casket of my Soul.

VOCABULARY (Students copy definitions from the mini dictionary at the end of the book.)

Recite and Copy Each Word	Write the Definition
embalmer	
benign	
embowered	
enshaded	
divine	
soothest	

Recite and Copy Each Word	Write the Definition
poppy	
lulling	
charities	
breeding	
woes	
conscience	
lords	
deftly	
wards	
seal	
casket	
soul	

NARRATE THE POEM (Students write a summary of the poem in their own words.)

_____

_____

_____

_____

_____

_____

_____

COPY THE EXCERPT (Students copy the provided poem excerpt.)

O soothest Sleep! if so it please thee, close
In midst of this thine hymn my willing eyes.

_____

_____

_____

_____

NARRATE THE EXCERPT (Students write a summary of the excerpt in their own words.)

DICTATE THE EXCERPT (Instructors recite the excerpt, and students write the words.)

DRAW THE POEM (Students create a visual representation of the poem.)

Poem Title:	Poem Author:

ELEMENTARY POETRY VOLUME 4: ADVANCING IN POETRY

POET VIII: WALT WHITMAN
LESSON 29. "A NOISELESS PATIENT SPIDER"

POET OVERVIEW

- Walt Whitman was born in 1819 in West Hills, New York.
- Whitman was one of nine children. His childhood was turbulent as his parents moved frequently due to financial difficulties.
- Whitman started working as a law office boy when he was only eleven years old.
- Whitman later became a printer's devil (apprentice) at a newspaper. He later taught, founded his own newspaper, served as a nurse during the Civil War, and performed a variety of other jobs.
- Whitman began publishing poetry as a teenager and continued through his life, determined to be a poet.
- Whitman spent 33 years perfecting his well-known poetry collection, *Leaves of Grass*.
- Whitman died of pleurisy in Camden, New Jersey at the age of 72.

COLOR THE POET

MAP THE POET

Locate and color Whitman's state of birth, **New York (NY)**, and state of death, **New Jersey (NJ)**, on the map of the United States.

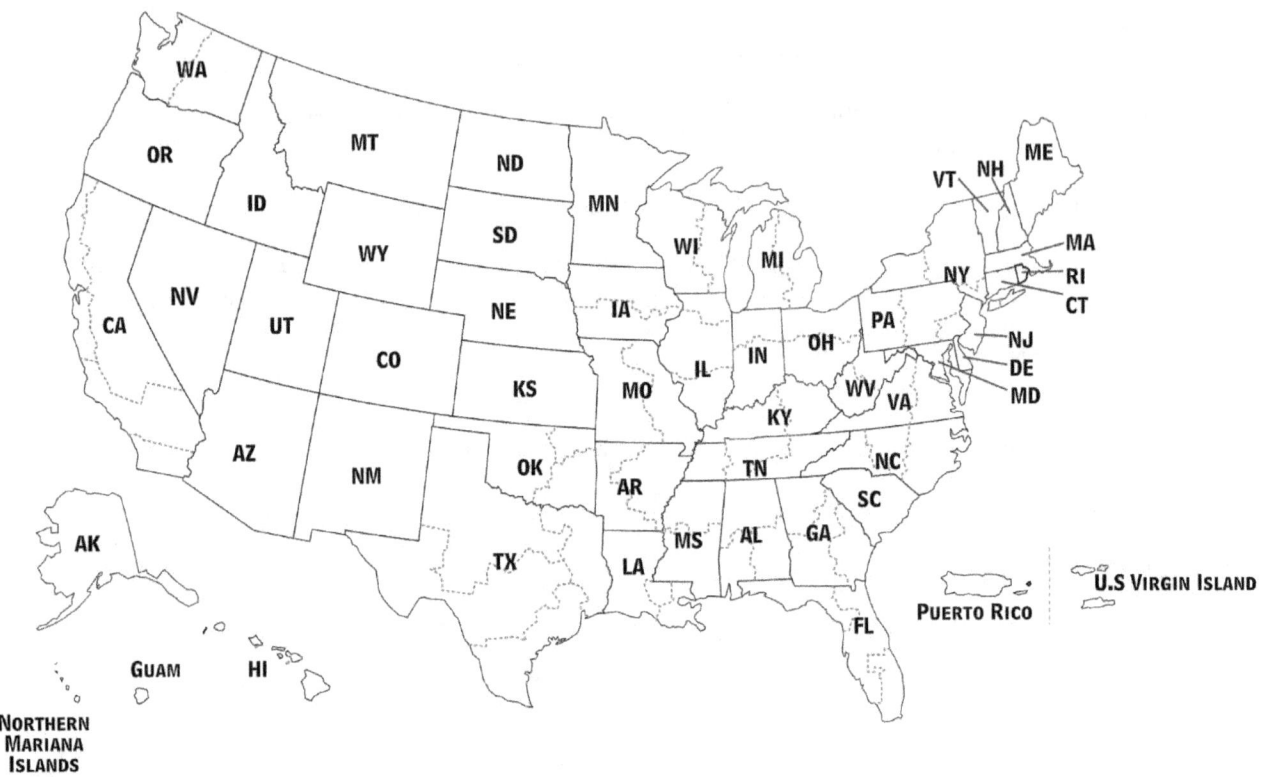

FEATURED POEM

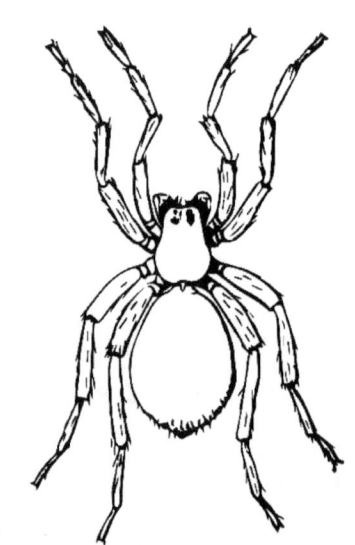

    A noiseless patient spider,

    I mark'd where on a little promontory it stood isolated,

    Mark'd how to explore the vacant vast surrounding,

    It launch'd forth filament, filament, filament, out of itself,

    Ever unreeling them, ever tirelessly speeding them.

    And you O my soul where you stand,

    Surrounded, detached, in measureless oceans of space,

    Ceaselessly musing, venturing, throwing, seeking the spheres to connect them,

    Till the bridge you will need be form'd, till the ductile anchor hold,

    Till the gossamer thread you fling catch somewhere, O my soul.

SYNOPSIS

In the first stanza of Walt Whitman's "A Noiseless Patient Spider," a spider launches its thread to explore an ocean rock. In the second stanza, Whitman compares the spinning spider to his seeking and exploring soul.

ENRICHMENT ACTIVITIES

1. **Recite Poem Information**
   Recite the title of the poem, the name of the poet, and the poem.

2. **Study the Poem Picture**
   Study the poem picture, and describe how it relates to the poem.

3. **Explore Poem Stanzas**
   - In poems, lines are often grouped together into stanzas, with space between them.
   - A stanza is a unit of a poem, written or printed as a paragraph; equivalent to a verse.
     - How many stanzas are in the lesson poem?
     - Compare and contrast the content of the stanzas of the lesson.

VOCABULARY (Students copy definitions from the mini dictionary at the end of the book.)

Recite and Copy Each Word	Write the Definition
noiseless	
patient	
promontory	
isolated	
vacant	
vast	
launched	

Recite and Copy Each Word	Write the Definition
filament	
detached	
measureless	
ceaselessly	
musing	
venturing	
spheres	
ductile	
anchor	
gossamer	
fling	
soul	

NARRATE THE POEM (Students write a summary of the poem in their own words.)

COPY THE EXCERPT (Students copy the provided poem excerpt.)

It launched forth filament, filament, filament, out of itself
Ever unreeling them, ever tirelessly speeding them

NARRATE THE EXCERPT (Students write a summary of the excerpt in their own words.)

DICTATE THE EXCERPT (Instructors recite the excerpt, and students write the words.)

ELEMENTARY POETRY VOLUME 4: ADVANCING IN POETRY

DRAW THE POEM (Students create a visual representation of the poem.)

Poem Title:	Poem Author:

SONJA GLUMICH

LESSON 30. "LONGINGS FOR HOME" BY WALT WHITMAN

FEATURED POEM

O Magnet South! O glistening, perfumed South! My South!

O quick mettle, rich blood, impulse, and love! Good and evil! O all dear to me!

O dear to me my birth-things—All moving things, and the trees where I was born—the grains, plants, rivers;

Dear to me my own slow sluggish rivers where they flow, distant, over flats of silvery sands, or through swamps;

Dear to me the Roanoke, the Savannah, the Altamahaw, the Pedee, the Tombigbee, the Santee, the Coosa, and the Sabine;

O pensive, far away wandering, I return with my Soul to haunt their banks again;

Again in Florida I float on transparent lakes—I float on the Okeechobee—I cross the hummock land, or through pleasant openings, or dense forests;

I see the parrots in the woods—I see the papaw tree and the blossoming titi;

Again, sailing in my coaster, on deck, I coast off Georgia—I coast up the Carolinas,

I see where the live-oak is growing—I see where the yellow-pine, the scented bay-tree, the lemon and orange, the cypress, the graceful palmetto;

I pass rude sea-headlands and enter Pamlico Sound through an inlet, and dart my vision inland;

O the cotton plant! the growing fields of rice, sugar, hemp!

The cactus, guarded with thorns—the laurel-tree, with large white flowers;

The range afar—the richness and barrenness—the old woods charged with mistletoe and trailing moss,

The piney odor and the gloom—the awful natural stillness, (Here in these dense swamps the freebooter carries his gun, and the fugitive slave has his conceal'd hut;)

O the strange fascination of these half-known, half-impassable swamps, infested by reptiles, resounding with the bellow of the alligator, the sad noises of the night-owl and the wild-cat, and the whirr of the rattlesnake;

The mocking-bird, the American mimic, singing all the forenoon—singing through the moon-lit night,

The humming-bird, the wild turkey, the raccoon, the opossum;

A Tennessee corn-field—the tall, graceful, long-leav'd corn—slender, flapping, bright green with tassels—with beautiful ears, each well-sheath'd in its husk;

An Arkansas prairie—a sleeping lake, or still bayou;

O my heart! O tender and fierce pangs—I can stand them not—I will depart;

O to be a Virginian, where I grew up! O to be a Carolinian!

O longings irrepressible! O I will go back to old Tennessee, and never wander more!

SYNOPSIS

Walt Whitman's "Longings for Home," describes the narrator's yearning for his southern homeland.

ENRICHMENT ACTIVITIES

1. **Recite Poem Information**
   Recite the title of the poem, the name of the poet, and the poem.

2. **Study the Poem Pictures**
   Study the poem pictures, and describe how they relate to the poem.

3. **Describe Your Home**
   - Describe what you like about the place you consider home.
   - Are there any places you especially enjoy visiting in your home area?
   - Are there any special rivers, plants, animals, or landmarks that characterize your home area?

4. **Color the Poem Map**
   Color the following states mentioned in the poem:
   - Georgia (GA) - Red
   - The Carolinas (NC, SC) – Blue, Yellow
   - Florida (FL) - Pink
   - Tennessee (TN) - Green
   - Arkansas (AR) - Purple
   - Virginia (VA) - Orange

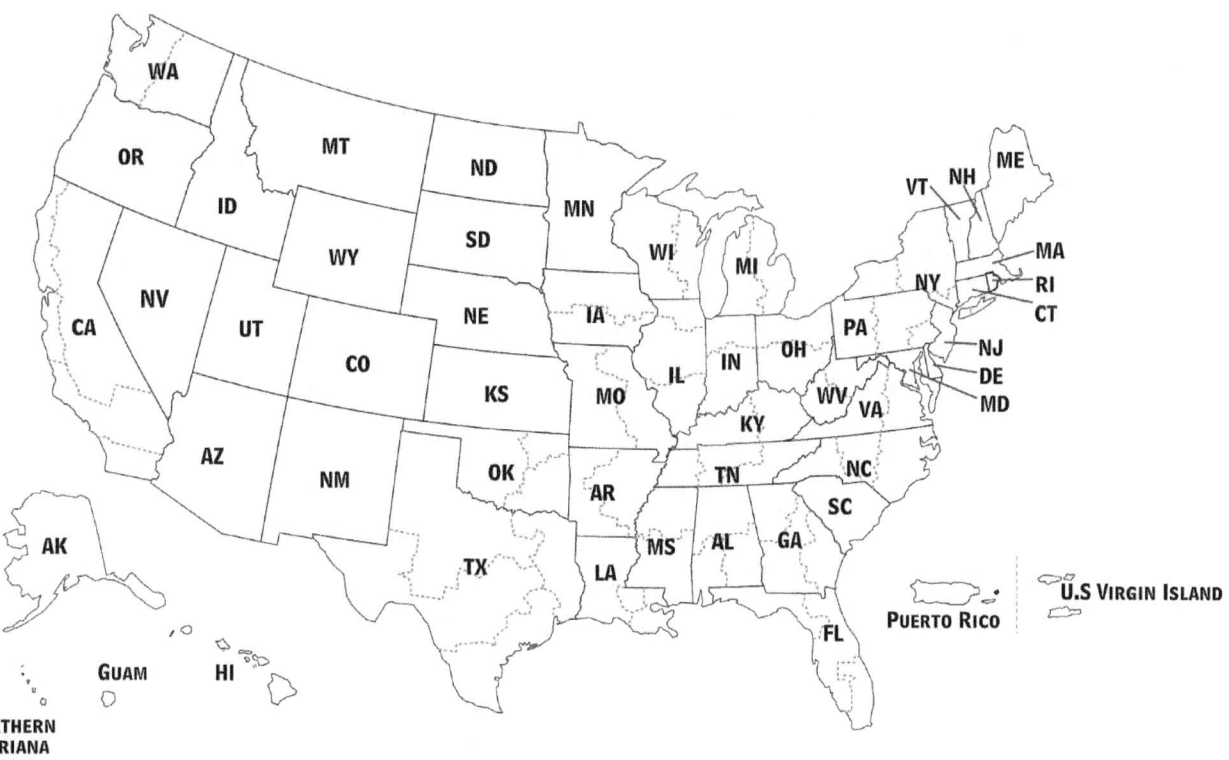

VOCABULARY (Students copy definitions from the mini dictionary at the end of the book.)

Recite and Copy Each Word	Write the Definition
magnet	
glistening	
perfumed	
south	
mettle	
impulse	
sluggish	
pensive	
transparent	
hummock	
inlet	
dart	

Recite and Copy Each Word	Write the Definition
barrenness	
half-impassable	
infested	
bellow	
sheath'd (sheathed)	
bayou	
pangs	
irrepressible	

NARRATE THE POEM (Students write a summary of the poem in their own words.)

COPY THE EXCERPT (Students copy the provided poem excerpt.)

O dear to me my birth-things—All moving things, and the trees where I was born—the grains, plants, rivers.

NARRATE THE EXCERPT (Students write a summary of the excerpt in their own words.)

DICTATE THE EXCERPT (Instructors recite the excerpt, and students write the words.)

DRAW THE POEM (Students create a visual representation of the poem.)

Poem Title:	Poem Author:

LESSON 31. "NIGHT ON THE PRAIRIES" BY WALT WHITMAN

FEATURED POEM

Night on the prairies;

The supper is over--the fire on the ground burns low;

The wearied emigrants sleep, wrapt in their blankets:

I walk by myself--I stand and look at the stars, which I think now I never realized before.

Now I absorb immortality and peace,

I admire death, and test propositions.

How plenteous! How spiritual! How resumé!

The same Old Man and Soul--the same old aspirations, and the same content.

I was thinking the day most splendid, till I saw what the not-day exhibited,

I was thinking this globe enough, till there sprang out so noiseless around me myriads of other globes.

Now, while the great thoughts of space and eternity fill me, I will measure myself by them;

And now, touch'd with the lives of other globes, arrived as far along as those of the earth,

Or waiting to arrive, or pass'd on farther than those of the earth,

I henceforth no more ignore them, than I ignore my own life,

Or the lives of the earth arrived as far as mine, or waiting to arrive.

O I see now that life cannot exhibit all to me--as the day cannot,

I see that I am to wait for what will be exhibited by death.

SYNOPSIS

Walt Whitman's "Night on the Prairies," is one of the poems found in his *Leaves of Grass* collection. In the poem, the narrator leaves his travelling companions sleeping around the fire to take a walk under the star-filled night sky. There he ponders his day and contemplates life, death, existence, eternity, and the myriad of other worlds that surround him. The narrator realizes that just as the day cannot show all there is to see and know after nightfall, life cannot show all there is to see and know after death.

ENRICHMENT ACTIVITIES

1. **Recite Poem Information**
   Recite the title of the poem, the name of the poet, and the poem.

2. **Study the Poem Picture**
   Study the poem picture, and describe how it relates to the poem.

3. **Revisit Poem Stanzas**
   - In poems, lines are often grouped together into stanzas, with space between them.
   - A stanza is a unit of a poem, written or printed as a paragraph; equivalent to a verse.
     - How many stanzas are in the lesson poem?
     - Describe what occurs in the fourth stanza.

VOCABULARY (Students copy definitions from the mini dictionary at the end of the book.)

Recite and Copy Each Word	Write the Definition
prairies	
wearied	
emigrants	
immortality	
peace	
admire	

Recite and Copy Each Word	Write the Definition
propositions	
plenteous	
spiritual	
resumé	
aspirations	
splendid	
exhibited	
sprang	
myriads	
eternity	
globes	
henceforth	

NARRATE THE POEM (Students write a summary of the poem in their own words.)

COPY THE EXCERPT (Students copy the provided poem excerpt.)

I walk by myself--I stand and look at the stars, which I think now I never realized before.

NARRATE THE EXCERPT (Students write a summary of the excerpt in their own words.)

DICTATE THE EXCERPT (Instructors recite the excerpt, and students write the words.)

DRAW THE POEM (Students create a visual representation of the poem.)

Poem Title:	Poem Author:

LESSON 32. "PIONEERS! O PIONEERS!" BY WALT WHITMAN

FEATURED POEM

Come my tan-faced children,
Follow well in order, get your weapons ready,
Have you your pistols? have you your sharp-edged axes?
Pioneers! O pioneers!

For we cannot tarry here,
We must march my darlings, we must bear the brunt of danger,
We the youthful sinewy races, all the rest on us depend,
Pioneers! O pioneers!

O you youths, Western youths,
So impatient, full of action, full of manly pride and friendship,
Plain I see you Western youths, see you tramping with the foremost,
Pioneers! O pioneers!

Have the elder races halted?
Do they droop and end their lesson, wearied over there beyond the seas?
We take up the task eternal, and the burden and the lesson,
Pioneers! O pioneers!

All the past we leave behind,
We debouch upon a newer mightier world, varied world,
Fresh and strong the world we seize, world of labor and the march,
Pioneers! O pioneers!

We detachments steady throwing,
Down the edges, through the passes, up the mountains steep,
Conquering, holding, daring, venturing as we go the unknown ways,
Pioneers! O pioneers!

We primeval forests felling,

We the rivers stemming, vexing we and piercing deep the mines within,

We the surface broad surveying, we the virgin soil upheaving,

Pioneers! O pioneers!

Colorado men are we,

From the peaks gigantic, from the great sierras and the high plateaus,

From the mine and from the gully, from the hunting trail we come,

Pioneers! O pioneers!

From Nebraska, from Arkansas,

Central inland race are we, from Missouri, with the continental blood intervein'd,

All the hands of comrades clasping, all the Southern, all the Northern,

Pioneers! O pioneers!

O resistless restless race!

O beloved race in all! O my breast aches with tender love for all!

O I mourn and yet exult, I am rapt with love for all,

Pioneers! O pioneers!

Raise the mighty mother mistress,

Waving high the delicate mistress, over all the starry mistress, (bend your heads all,)

Raise the fang'd and warlike mistress, stern, impassive, weapon'd mistress,

Pioneers! O pioneers!

See my children, resolute children,

By those swarms upon our rear we must never yield or falter,

Ages back in ghostly millions frowning there behind us urging,

Pioneers! O pioneers!

On and on the compact ranks,

With accessions ever waiting, with the places of the dead quickly fill'd,

Through the battle, through defeat, moving yet and never stopping,

Pioneers! O pioneers!

O to die advancing on!

Are there some of us to droop and die? has the hour come?

Then upon the march we fittest die, soon and sure the gap is fill'd.

Pioneers! O pioneers!

All the pulses of the world,

Falling in they beat for us, with the Western movement beat,

Holding single or together, steady moving to the front, all for us,

Pioneers! O pioneers!

Life's involv'd and varied pageants,

All the forms and shows, all the workmen at their work,

All the seamen and the landsmen, all the masters with their slaves,

Pioneers! O pioneers!

All the hapless silent lovers,

All the prisoners in the prisons, all the righteous and the wicked,

All the joyous, all the sorrowing, all the living, all the dying,

Pioneers! O pioneers!

I too with my soul and body,

We, a curious trio, picking, wandering on our way,

Through these shores amid the shadows, with the apparitions pressing,

Pioneers! O pioneers!

Lo, the darting bowling orb!

Lo, the brother orbs around, all the clustering suns and planets,

All the dazzling days, all the mystic nights with dreams,

Pioneers! O pioneers!

These are of us, they are with us,

All for primal needed work, while the followers there in embryo wait behind,

We today's procession heading, we the route for travel clearing,

Pioneers! O pioneers!

O you daughters of the West!

O you young and elder daughters! O you mothers and you wives!

Never must you be divided, in our ranks you move united,

Pioneers! O pioneers!

Minstrels latent on the prairies!

(Shrouded bards of other lands, you may rest, you have done your work,)

Soon I hear you coming warbling, soon you rise and tramp amid us,

Pioneers! O pioneers!

Not for delectations sweet,

Not the cushion and the slipper, not the peaceful and the studious,

Not the riches safe and palling, not for us the tame enjoyment,

Pioneers! O pioneers!

Do the feasters gluttonous feast?

Do the corpulent sleepers sleep? have they lock'd and bolted doors?

Still be ours the diet hard, and the blanket on the ground,

Pioneers! O pioneers!

Has the night descended?

Was the road of late so toilsome? did we stop discouraged nodding on our way?

Yet a passing hour I yield you in your tracks to pause oblivious,

Pioneers! O pioneers!

Till with sound of trumpet,

Far, far off the daybreak call—hark! how loud and clear I hear it wind,

Swift! to the head of the army!--swift! spring to your places,

Pioneers! O pioneers!

SYNOPSIS

Walt Whitman's "Pioneers! O Pioneers!" is one of the poems found in his *Leaves of Grass* collection. In the poem, the narrator calls on the brave, the strong, and the determined pioneers to make the journey to the American West to claim their destinies.

ENRICHMENT ACTIVITIES

1. **Recite Poem Information**
   Recite the title of the poem, the name of the poet, and the poem.

2. **Study the Poem Pictures**
   Study the poem pictures, and describe how they relate to the poem.

3. **Revisit Poem Stanzas**
   - In poems, lines are often grouped together into stanzas, with space between them.
   - A stanza is a unit of a poem, written or printed as a paragraph; equivalent to a verse.
     o Pick one stanza from the poem that is your favorite.
     o Describe why you like this stanza the best.

VOCABULARY (Students copy definitions from the mini dictionary at the end of the book.)

Recite and Copy Each Word	Write the Definition
pioneers	
tarry	
brunt	
sinewy	
tramping	
elder	

Recite and Copy Each Word	Write the Definition
eternal	
debouch	
detachments	
primeval	
felling	
vexing	
plateaus	
gully	
continental	
exult	
rapt	
impassive	

NARRATE THE POEM (Students write a summary of the poem in their own words.)

COPY THE EXCERPT (Students copy the provided poem excerpt.)

Through the battle, through defeat, moving yet and never stopping,
Pioneers! O pioneers!

NARRATE THE EXCERPT (Students write a summary of the excerpt in their own words.)

DICTATE THE EXCERPT (Instructors recite the excerpt, and students write the words.)

DRAW THE POEM (Students create a visual representation of the poem.)

Poem Title:	Poem Author:

POET IX: ELIZABETH BARRETT BROWNING
LESSON 33. "HOW DO I LOVE THEE?"

POET OVERVIEW

- Elizabeth Barrett Browning was born in 1806 in Kelloe, Durham, England (United Kingdom).
- Elizabeth was the eldest of twelve children. She had health problems growing up, including lung problems and pain in her neck.
- Elizabeth wrote her first poems at around age six and published her first collection of poems at around age 32.
- Elizabeth became well-known as a poet while still alive.
- Elizabeth married Robert Browning, another famous poet, in secret, for they feared her father's disapproval. When Elizabeth's father found out about the marriage, he disinherited her.
- Elizabeth and Robert moved to Italy, where she lived out her life.
- Elizabeth died of an unknown illness in Florence, Italy at the age of 55.

COLOR THE POET

MAP THE POET

Locate and color Barrett Browning's country of birth, **England (United Kingdom)**, and country of death, **Italy**, on the map of Europe.

FEATURED POEM

How do I love thee? Let me count the ways.

I love thee to the depth and breadth and height

My soul can reach, when feeling out of sight

For the ends of being and ideal grace.

I love thee to the level of every day's

Most quiet need, by sun and candle-light.

I love thee freely, as men strive for right.

I love thee purely, as they turn from praise.

I love thee with the passion put to use

In my old griefs, and with my childhood's faith.

I love thee with a love I seemed to lose

With my lost saints. I love thee with the breath,

Smiles, tears, of all my life; and, if God choose,

I shall but love thee better after death.

SYNOPSIS

Elizabeth Barrett Browning's "How Do I Love Thee?" attempts to quantify and express the depth of the narrator's love for another.

ENRICHMENT ACTIVITIES

1. **Recite Poem Information**
   Recite the title of the poem, the name of the poet, and the poem.

2. **Study the Poem Picture**
   Study the poem picture, and describe how it relates to the poem.

3. **Describe Your Love for Someone**
   - Describe your love for someone special.
   - Compare the magnitude of your love to something else, such as the highest mountain, the brightest supernova, or the deepest ocean trench.

VOCABULARY (Students copy definitions from the mini dictionary at the end of the book.)

Recite and Copy Each Word	Write the Definition
thee	
depth	
breadth	
height	
grace	
strive	
purely	
praise	
saints	

NARRATE THE POEM (Students write a summary of the poem in their own words.)

COPY THE EXCERPT (Students copy the provided poem excerpt.)

How do I love thee? Let me count the ways.
I love thee to the depth and breadth and height
My soul can reach, when feeling out of sight

NARRATE THE EXCERPT (Students write a summary of the excerpt in their own words.)

DICTATE THE EXCERPT (Instructors recite the excerpt, and students write the words.)

DRAW THE POEM (Students create a visual representation of the poem.)

Poem Title:	Poem Author:

LESSON 34. "THE BEST THING IN THE WORLD" BY ELIZABETH BARRETT BROWNING

FEATURED POEM

What's the best thing in the world?

June-rose, by May-dew impearled;

Sweet south-wind, that means no rain;

Truth, not cruel to a friend;

Pleasure, not in haste to end;

Beauty, not self-decked and curled

Till its pride is over-plain;

Light, that never makes you wink;

Memory, that gives no pain;

Love, when, so, you're loved again.

What's the best thing in the world?

— Something out of it, I think.

SYNOPSIS

Elizabeth Barrett Browning's "The Best Thing in the World" describes candidates for the best thing in the world and then concludes that perhaps the best thing is something not of this world.

ENRICHMENT ACTIVITIES

1. **Recite Poem Information**
   Recite the title of the poem, the name of the poet, and the poem.

2. **Study the Poem Picture**
   Study the poem picture, and describe how it relates to the poem.

3. **Describe Your "Best Thing in the World"**
   - What is your best thing in the world?
   - Why is it your best thing in the world?

VOCABULARY (Students copy definitions from the mini dictionary at the end of the book.)

Recite and Copy Each Word	Write the Definition
impearled	
cruel	
haste	
self-decked	
pride	

NARRATE THE POEM (Students write a summary of the poem in their own words.)

_____

_____

_____

_____

_____

_____

COPY THE EXCERPT (Students copy the provided poem excerpt.)

What's the best thing in the world?
— Something out of it, I think.

_____

_____

_____

_____

NARRATE THE EXCERPT (Students write a summary of the excerpt in their own words.)

DICTATE THE EXCERPT (Instructors recite the excerpt, and students write the words.)

DRAW THE POEM (Students create a visual representation of the poem.)

Poem Title:	Poem Author:

LESSON 35. "THE MUSICAL INSTRUMENT"
BY ELIZABETH BARRETT BROWNING

FEATURED POEM

I. What was he doing, the great god Pan,
Down in the reeds by the river?
Spreading ruin and scattering ban,
Splashing and paddling with hoofs of a goat,
And breaking the golden lilies afloat
With the dragon-fly on the river.

II. He tore out a reed, the great god Pan,
From the deep cool bed of the river:
The limpid water turbidly ran,
And the broken lilies a-dying lay,
And the dragon-fly had fled away,
Ere he brought it out of the river.

III. High on the shore sate the great god Pan,
While turbidly flowed the river;
And hacked and hewed as a great god can,
With his hard bleak steel at the patient reed,
Till there was not a sign of a leaf indeed
To prove it fresh from the river.

IV. He cut it short, did the great god Pan,
(How tall it stood in the river!)
Then drew the pith, like the heart of a man,
Steadily from the outside ring,
And notched the poor dry empty thing
In holes, as he sate by the river.

V. This is the way, laughed the great god Pan,
(Laughed while he sate by the river,)
The only way, since gods began
To make sweet music, they could succeed.
Then, dropping his mouth to a hole in the reed,
He blew in power by the river.

VI. Sweet, sweet, sweet, O Pan!
Piercing sweet by the river!
Blinding sweet, O great god Pan!
The sun on the hill forgot to die,
And the lilies revived, and the dragonfly
Came back to dream on the river.

VII. Yet half a beast is the great god Pan,
To laugh as he sits by the river,
Making a poet out of a man:
The true gods sigh for the cost and pain, —
For the reed which grows nevermore again
As a reed with the reeds in the river.

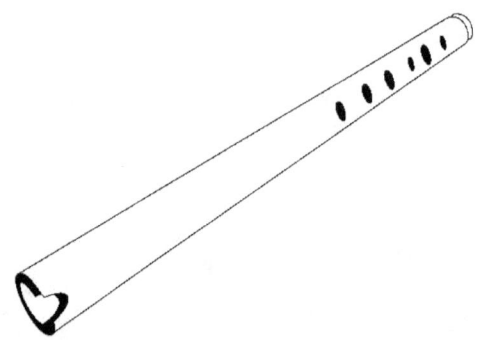

SYNOPSIS

Elizabeth Barrett Browning's "The Musical Instrument" describes Pan, the mythological half-human and half-goat, making and playing a reed down by a river. Pan makes beautiful music, but it comes at the cost of the life of the reed, which grows no more.

ENRICHMENT ACTIVITIES

1. **Recite Poem Information**
   Recite the title of the poem, the name of the poet, and the poem.

2. **Study the Poem Pictures**
   Study the poem pictures, and describe how they relate to the poem.

3. **Discuss the Costs of Creating Things**
   - The poem remarks how the cost of the beautiful music was the life of the reed.
   - Describe the benefits and costs of creating the following items:
     o A bouquet of flowers
     o A piece of furniture
     o A house
     o A shirt
     o A breakfast

VOCABULARY (Students copy definitions from the mini dictionary at the end of the book.)

Recite and Copy Each Word	Write the Definition
Pan	
reeds	
ruin	
ban	
limpid	
turbidly	
sate	
hewed	
pith	
notched	

NARRATE THE POEM (Students write a summary of the poem in their own words.)

COPY THE EXCERPT (Students copy the provided poem excerpt.)

He cut it short, did the great god Pan,
(How tall it stood in the river!)
And notched the poor dry empty thing
In holes, as he sate by the river.

NARRATE THE EXCERPT (Students write a summary of the excerpt in their own words.)

DICTATE THE EXCERPT (Instructors recite the excerpt, and students write the words.)

DRAW THE POEM (Students create a visual representation of the poem.)

Poem Title:	Poem Author:

LESSON 36. "CHANGE UPON CHANGE" BY ELIZABETH BARRETT BROWNING

FEATURED POEM

>Five months ago the stream did flow,
>The lilies bloomed within the sedge,
>And we were lingering to and fro,
>Where none will track thee in this snow,
>Along the stream, beside the hedge.
>Ah, Sweet, be free to love and go!
>For if I do not hear thy foot,
>The frozen river is as mute,
>The flowers have dried down to the root:
>And why, since these be changed since May,
>Shouldst thou change less than they.
>
>And slow, slow as the winter snow
>The tears have drifted to mine eyes;
>And my poor cheeks, five months ago
>Set blushing at thy praises so,
>Put paleness on for a disguise.
>Ah, Sweet, be free to praise and go!
>For if my face is turned too pale,
>It was thine oath that first did fail, --
>It was thy love proved false and frail, --
>And why, since these be changed enow,
>Should I change less than thou.

SYNOPSIS

Elizabeth Barrett Browning's "Change Upon Change" compares the change from spring to winter with the cessation of love. For example, in the spring, rivers (i.e. love) rush and in the winter, rivers still.

ENRICHMENT ACTIVITIES

1. **Recite Poem Information**
   Recite the title of the poem, the name of the poet, and the poem.

2. **Study the Poem Picture**
   Study the poem picture, and describe how it relates to the poem.

3. **Discuss Winter Versus Spring**
   - List several differences between winter and spring.
   - Describe why you prefer either winter or spring.

VOCABULARY (Students copy definitions from the mini dictionary at the end of the book.)

Recite and Copy Each Word	Write the Definition
sedge	
lingering	
thee	
hedge	
thy	
mute	
thou	

NARRATE THE POEM (Students write a summary of the poem in their own words.)

COPY THE EXCERPT (Students copy the provided poem excerpt.)

The frozen river is as mute,
The flowers have dried down to the root:
And why, since these be changed since May,
Shouldst thou change less than they.

NARRATE THE EXCERPT (Students write a summary of the excerpt in their own words.)

DICTATE THE EXCERPT (Instructors recite the excerpt, and students write the words.)

DRAW THE POEM (Students create a visual representation of the poem.)

Poem Title:	Poem Author:

ELEMENTARY POETRY VOLUME 4: ADVANCING IN POETRY

MINI DICTIONARY

Note – This book provides definitions in context of provided vocabulary words and their encompassing poems. Additional definitions for terms other than those provided often exist.

Word	Definition
abash	To make ashamed; to embarrass.
ablution	The act of washing something.
abode	A residence, dwelling or habitation.
abyss	A bottomless depth.
aches	Suffers pain.
admires	Looks upon with pleasure or delight.
admiring	Looking upon with pleasure or delight.
advertise	To give information about a person or goods and services to gain attention.
affinity	A natural attraction.
aghast	Terrified, shocked, or horrified.
aground	Resting on the bottom.
alas	Used to express sadness or regret.
alders	Any of several trees or shrubs belonging to the birch family.
aloft	At, to, or in the air or sky.
alter	To become different.
amethyst	1. A purple color. 2. A transparent purple variety of gemstone.
amid	Surrounded by; in the middle of.
anchor	Hold an object to a fixed point.
anchored	Held an object to a fixed point.
arches	Items having an inverted U shape, such as bridges.
arms	Weapons.
aspires	Hopes or dreams; longs for; tries to reach.
aspirations	Passionate wishes or desires.
astray	In a wrong direction.
atmosphere	1. The air in a particular place. 2. The apparent mood felt in an environment.
averse	Having a dislike of or opposition to something.
awakenings	Realizations or discoveries.
baffles	Confuses or puzzles.
ban	To curse.
bark	A small sailing vessel, such as a rowing boat.
barrack	A building for soldiers.
barrenness	1. Desolation or emptiness. 2. Lack of vegetation.
bay	A body of water surrounded on three sides by land.
bayou	A swamp or stagnant creek or river.

Word	Definition
beguile	To charm or delight.
belfry	A steeple or tower containing bells.
believed	Accepted as true.
bellow	The deep roar of an animal.
benign	Kind and gentle.
beside	Next to.
blush	Turn pink or red.
bodice	The upper part of a women's dress.
bog	A marsh or swamp.
borne	Supported, carried, or survived.
bosom	The chest of a human.
bosom-friend	A very close friend.
Botticelli	Sandro Botticelli, Italian painter.
bough	Firm branch of a tree.
boughs	Firm branches of a tree.
bourn	A small stream or brook.
breadth	The measure of how wide something is.
breeding	Growing or multiplying.
bridle	The headgear with which a horse is directed.
brunt	The full negative effects of.
buoyant	1. Able to float. 2. Lighthearted and lively.
cage	An enclosure made of bars.
carriage	A wheeled vehicle, generally drawn by horses.
casket	A coffin.
ceasing	Stopping.
ceaselessly	Without stopping.
cellar	An enclosed underground space used for storage or shelter.
cells	Sections of a larger structure.
centuries	Periods of 100 consecutive years.
charities	Activities that help those in need.
chillest	The coldest.
choir	A group of people or animals who sing or make noise together.
chord	A pleasant-sounding group of three or more notes heard as if sounding simultaneously.
chuckles	Quiet laughs.
cider-press	A machine that presses juice from apples to make cider.
cinctured	Enclosed or encircled.
civility	Politeness.
clammy	Cold and damp.
clasps	Holds or grasps.
clew (clue)	Information that leads to understanding.

Word	Definition
clings	Holds tightly.
cobbles	Short for cobblestones.
cobblestones	Rounded stones from a river bed, used for paving roads.
comfort	Something relieving suffering or worry.
companions	Friends with whom one spends time.
conscience	The sense of right or wrong that affects one's own behavior.
conspiring	Secretly making plans to bring bad or illegal results.
continental	Of or relating to a continent.
copse	A thicket of small trees or shrubs.
core	The heart or inner part of a thing.
cornice	A part projecting from walls of a building, used to direct rainwater away from the walls.
countenance	Appearance or facial expression.
crescent	The view of the moon in its first or last quarter, with ends terminating in points.
crinkled	Bent or crumpled.
crocus	A flowering plant with blooms that are often purple.
croft	A fenced piece of land.
cruel	Mean or heartless.
curlew	Any of several wading birds with long, slender, downcurved bills.
cut	To divide a deck of playing cards.
dais	A raised platform or table in a room.
darksome	Characterized by darkness and gloom.
dart	A sudden or fast movement.
dazzle	To confuse the sight with bright light.
debouch	To emerge from a narrow place into open country or a wider space.
defiance	A challenging attitude or behavior.
deftly	Skillfully, quickly, and neatly in action.
dense	1. Compact or crowded together. 2. Thick or allowing little light to pass through.
depth	The deepest part.
descended	Moved downward.
descends	Moves downward.
detached	Moved apart from.
detachments	Smaller groups split off from the main group.
dew	Moisture in the air that settles on plants or other objects as drops of water.
dint	A mark or indentation.
disused	Not used or neglected.
divine	Beautiful, holy, or heavenly.
dodge	To avoid by moving quickly out of the way.
dome	Anything shaped like an upside-down bowl.

Word	Definition
doth	An archaic term for "do" or "does."
doubtless	Free from doubt. Certain.
down	Soft, fluffy immature feathers which grow on young birds.
dream	A hope or wish.
dreary	Drab, colorless, or cheerless.
drifting	Moving slowly, especially pushed by currents of water or air.
drone	A monotone or unchanging sound.
drowsed	Slept.
drowsing	Sleeping.
ductile	Capable of being stretched into thin wire without breaking.
dusty	Covered with dust.
dwell	To reside or live.
ease	Comfortable or relaxed.
edged	Bordered by a certain material, color, and so on.
efface	To erase.
elder	Older.
embalmer	One who prepares a corpse for burial.
embowered	Enclosed or protected something.
embrown	To make brown.
emerald	Of a rich green color.
emigrants	People who leave a country to settle in a new country.
encampment	A campsite.
enchant	1. To attract and delight, to charm. 2. To cast a spell upon.
enshaded	Kept in shade or darkness.
equipoise	A state of balance.
ere	Before.
eremite	A hermit; a religious recluse, someone who lives alone.
errands	Journeys undertaken to accomplish tasks.
essence	Fragrance, a perfume.
estates	Land and often houses owned by particular individuals.
eternal	Lasting forever.
eternity	A period of time which lasts forever.
ethereal	1. Delicate, light and airy. 2. Spirit-like or otherworldly.
eve (eave)	The underside of a roof that extends beyond the external walls of a building.
examine	To inspect carefully.
exhibited	Displayed or showed.
extended	Straightened or held out.
extremity	The most extreme or furthest point of something.
exult	To rejoice.

Word	Definition
faint	Lacking strength.
fairer	More beautiful.
fancies	1. Imagination. 2. Images that form in the mind.
fathom	Understand.
fatigue	Tiredness.
felling	Chopping down.
festive	In the mood to celebrate.
filament	A fine thread.
fleet	Swift or quick.
fleurs-de-lys	Designs representing a flower whose three petals are joined together at the bottom.
fling	To throw.
forethought	Think about or plan ahead of time.
forevermore	Forever.
forsaken	Deserted, abandoned.
frigates	19th-century warships.
fruitfulness	The state of being favorable to the growth of fruit or vegetation.
furrow	A trench cut in the soil.
gale	A violent wind.
gapes	1. Opens the mouth wide. 2. Stares in wonder.
garments	Clothing.
gauze	Mist or haze.
gilded	Golden or covered with gold.
girth	A band passed under the belly of an animal, which holds a saddle in place.
gleam	A shaft, beam, or ray of light.
gleaner	One who gathers what is left in a field after a harvest.
glide	To move smoothly or effortlessly.
glistening	Sparkling, glinting, or flashing.
globes	Planets such as the earth.
gnats	Tiny insects that often gather in swarms.
gossamer	A delicate film as of cobwebs.
gourd	A hard-shelled fruit.
grace	1. Elegant movement or poise. 2. Charming, pleasing qualities.
granary	A storage facility for grain or animal feed.
grenadiers	Soldiers who throw grenades.
grief	Sadness or sorrow.
grins	Smiles in which the lips are parted to reveal the teeth.
guile	Deceit or dishonesty.

Word	Definition
gully	A small valley.
halcyon	Peaceful, calm, blissful, or serene.
half-impassable	Incapable of being crossed at many places.
haste	Speed or swiftness.
hasten	Speed up or move quickly.
hastens	Speeds up or moves quickly.
haunted	Of a location haunted by ghosts or spirits.
hedge	A thicket of bushes.
height	The highest point or maximum degree.
hempen	Related to ropes made of the hemp plant.
henceforth	From now on.
hewed	Chopped away at or whittled.
hoarded	Gathered a cache of valued objects.
hoary	Frosty.
hope	The belief or expectation that something wished for can or will happen.
host	A large number of items.
hostler	A person employed at an inn or stable to look after horses. A groom.
hue	1. Form or appearance. 2. A shade of color.
hummock	A small hill.
hushed	Quiet.
illuminated	Lit up.
imitative	Copying another thing.
immortality	The condition of living forever and never dying.
impalpable	Not able to be sensed.
impassive	1. Having or revealing no emotion. 2. Still or motionless.
impatient	Anxious or eager to begin something.
impearled	To decorate as if with pearls.
impetuous	Acting impulsively without care.
impressions	Effects or marks changing something.
impulse	A wish or urge.
infested	Plagued by large numbers of an invading force.
inlet	A body of water let into a coast, such as a bay or a cove.
inn	Any establishment where travelers can procure lodging, food, and drink.
inoffensive	Not causing anger, disgust, or hatred.
instep	The arched part of the top of the foot between the toes and the ankle.
invariably	Always; every time.
irrepressible	Uncontrollable.
isolated	Placed or standing apart or alone.
jar	A sense of alarm or dismay.
jocund	Merry and in high spirits. Happy.

Word	Definition
kernel	A single seed or grain, especially of corn or wheat.
kindled	Started a fire.
labour (labor)	Toil, work.
labored	Toiled, worked.
lad	A boy or young man.
laden	Weighted down with a load.
lag-last	One who comes in last.
lark	Any of a small, singing variety of birds.
larks	A small, singing variety of birds.
lass	A girl or young lady.
launched	Thrown or hurled.
lay	A ballad or sung poem.
leaflet	1. One part of a compound leaf. 2. A small plant leaf.
leisure	Time free from work or duties.
lies	To give false information with an intent to deceive.
lilies	Large, fragrant flowers that sprout from a tall stem.
limpid	Clear, transparent, or bright.
lingering	Waiting or remaining.
listless	Lacking energy, enthusiasm, or liveliness.
livelong	Total, complete, whole.
lone	Unfrequented by human beings; solitary.
longing	An earnest and deep desire.
lords	Possessing mastery or ownership.
lulling	Soothing or calming.
luxury	1. Very wealthy and comfortable surroundings. 2. Something very pleasant but not really needed in life.
lynx	Any of several medium-sized wild cats.
magnet	Something or someone that attracts other people or things.
magnified	Made to appear larger.
mantle	A cloak or open robe.
mar	To damage or spoil.
maturing	Aging, ripening, or growing.
mead	A meadow.
measureless	Unable to be measured.
mellow	1. Soft or tender by reason of ripeness. 2. Relaxed or calm.
mercury	A silvery-colored, toxic metal.
metaphor	The use of a word or phrase to refer to something that it is not to make an implied comparison.
mettle	A quality of endurance and courage.
misled	Led astray, tricked, or deceived.

Word	Definition
moorings	Places to secure vessels with a cables or anchors.
moors	An extensive wasteland covered with patches of heath, and having a poor, light soil, but sometimes marshy, and abounding in peat.
morn	Morning.
mortmain	The perpetual, inalienable possession of lands by a non-personal entity.
mourn	Express sadness or sorrow.
mourns	Expresses sadness or sorrow.
muffled	Stifled or covered up.
murmurs	Low or quiet sounds or speech.
musing	Thinking or contemplating.
muster	A collection of people or things.
musty	Having a stale odor.
mute	1. Not able to speak. 2. Silent.
myriad	Countless number.
myriads	Countless numbers.
mystic	1. Mysterious, strange, or enigmatic. 2. One who believes they can know the divine through contemplation.
nay	No.
nevermore	Never again.
nobody	1. No person; no one. 2. A person of no importance or authority.
noiseless	Creating no noise.
notch	Mark with a V-shaped cut or indent.
notched	Marked with a V-shaped cut or indent.
ode	A short poem, often written to honor someone or something.
o'er	Over.
oozing	Secreting, leaking, flowing, or seeping.
over-brimmed	Overflowed or spilled over.
over-wise (overwise)	Too clever for one's own good.
overflow	To flow over the brim of a container.
pair	Two of something.
Pan	Greek god of nature, often visualized as half goat and half man playing pipes.
pangs	Sharp, sudden feelings, as of joy or sorrow.
parterre	A garden with paths between flowerbeds.
patient	Willing to wait without losing one's temper.
patterned	Having a repeating arrangement of something such as shapes and/or colors.
peace	A state of tranquility, quiet, and harmony.
pendulum	A body suspended from a fixed support so that it swings freely back and forth under the influence of gravity.
pensive	Looking thoughtful or sad.

Word	Definition
perceives	Sees, aware of, understands.
perches	Rests or roosts, in some cases in an elevated position.
perfumed	Scented.
peril	Danger.
perpetual	Lasting forever.
perturbations	Disturbances.
phantoms	Spirits, ghosts, or apparitions.
pioneers	People who go before, as into the wilderness, preparing the way for others to follow.
pith	The soft, spongy substance in the center of the stems of many plants and trees.
plains	Relatively flat and empty expanses of land.
plaited	Folded.
planks	Long and broad pieces of wood.
plateaus	Largely level expanses of land at a high elevation.
plenteous	In great quantity; abundant.
poised	Suspended.
pomegranates	Fruit with red, seedy pulp and thick, hard, reddish skins.
poppy	A plant with red flowers containing sleep-inducing but addictive medicinal substances.
poppies	Plants with red flowers containing sleep-inducing but addictive medicinal substances.
port	A place on the coast at which ships can shelter or dock.
prairies	Extensive areas of relatively flat grassland with few, if any, trees.
praise	To speak highly of, to celebrate, or to glorify.
prayer	A practice of communicating with one's God or higher power.
precede	Go in front of.
prepense	Planned beforehand.
presuming	Taking for granted, sometimes mistakenly.
pricks	Pierces, punctures, or pokes a hole in something.
pride	An unreasonable feeling of superiority.
primeval	Ancient or prehistoric.
promontory	A cliff extending into a body of water.
propositions	Statements assumed to be true or false.
prospect	The potential things that may come to pass, often favorable.
public	Able to be seen or known by everyone; open to general view.
purely	1. Completely, wholly. 2. Innocently, chastely.
radiant	Radiating light and/or heat.
rapt	Enthusiastic or absorbed.
realm	An otherworldly, magical, or ethereal dimension or domain.
reaped	Cut or harvested.

Word	Definition
reeds	Tall stiff perennial grass-like plants growing in groups near water.
resolved	Determined.
resumé	Abstract or intangible.
ringed	Marked or surrounded by one or more rings, loops, or circles.
ripening	The process of maturing, sweetening, or becoming ready for harvest.
ripple	A moving disturbance, or undulation, in the surface of a fluid.
rises	Moves upwards.
robust	Strong, vigorous, or healthy.
root	The part of a plant, generally underground, that anchors the plant body and absorbs water and nutrients.
rude	Rough, harsh, or severe.
ruin	The state of being a ruin, destroyed or decayed.
russet	A reddish-brown color.
saints	1. People to whom a religious group has attributed the title of "saint"; holy or godly people. 2. People with positive qualities; one who does good.
sallows	A willow with broad leaves, large catkins, and tough wood.
sate	Archaic form of "sat."
scanned	Examined sequentially, part by part.
scarcely	Almost not at all; hardly.
scrutinizing	Examining something with great care.
seal	A tight closure, secure against leakage.
sedge	A plant with long grasslike leaves that often grows in dense tufts in marshy places.
seedling	A young plant.
seek	To search for.
seldom	Almost never, rarely.
self-decked	Dressed up or decorated by oneself.
sentinel	A guard or watchman.
settles	Sinks down or deposits.
shades	Shields from light.
shattered	Broke violently into small pieces.
sheath'd (sheathed)	Encased or covered.
shoot	The emerging stem and leaves of a new plant.
shoreward	In the direction of the shoreline.
shrills	To make a high-pitched and piercing noise.
shuffle	The act of rearranging the order of something.
sift	To examine carefully.
signal	A sign made to give notice of some occurrence, command, or danger.
silk	A fine, soft cloth woven from silk fibers.
sill	A horizontal slat which forms the base of a window.
sinewy	Strong, muscular, and powerful.

Word	Definition
sluggish	Slow, idle, or lazy.
sombre (somber)	Dark or dreary in character; joyless, and grim.
somebody	A recognized person, a celebrity.
soothest	To calm, ease pain, or relieve suffering.
soul	The spirit or essence of a person usually thought to consist of one's thoughts and personality.
south	One of the four major compass points, typically downwards on a map.
spar	Any beam-like structure on a ship.
spectral	Of, or pertaining to ghosts or specters.
spheres	Three-dimensional objects in which every cross-section is a circle.
spire	A tapering structure built on a roof or tower.
spiritual	Of or pertaining to the spirit or the soul.
splendid	Showy; magnificent; brilliant.
splendor	1. Great light, luster or brilliance. 2. Magnificent appearance, display or grandeur.
spoke	A support structure that connects the hub of a wheel to the rim.
sprang/sprung	Jumped or leaped.
stay	Stop or detain.
steadfast	Fixed or unchanging; steady.
stealthy	Acting secretly such that the actions are unnoticed by others.
steed	A male adult horse.
steeds	Male adult horses.
steeple	A tall tower.
stir	To move or disturb.
strangest	Oddest or least normal.
strife	Conflict or trouble.
strike	1. To hit. 2. To cause to sound by one or more beats.
strive	Try earnestly and persistently in the face of opposition.
strove	Tried earnestly and persistently in the face of opposition.
stubble	1. Short, coarse protrusions. 2. The short stalks left in a field after crops have been harvested.
subtleties	Instances of being not obvious or easily understood.
sum	A total quantity obtained by addition or collection.
surmised	Guessed.
surroundings	The environment or areas around something.
swath	1. The track cut out by a scythe in mowing. 2. A broad sweep or expanse.
sweeping	To travel quickly.
swoon	To faint or lose consciousness.
tarry	To delay or linger.
tempests	Storms.

Word	Definition
tender	Gentle or sweet.
thatch	A roof or covering made of interwoven straw, rushes, reeds, or leaves.
thee	Archaic version of "you."
thickset	Stout or plump.
thou	Archaic version of "you."
thrive	To grow vigorously.
thronged	Full of things crowded together; swarming.
thrusts	Juts or pushes up.
thy	Archaic version of "your."
tide	The periodic change of the sea level, caused by the gravitational influence of the sun and the moon.
tinctured	Colored.
tireless	Never tiring or fatigued.
title-deeds	Documents by which the titles to property are transferred between parties.
to and fro	Back and forth; with an alternating motion.
toil	Hard work, especially of a grueling nature.
tone	A specific pitch of a musical sound.
tortured	Tormented or in agony.
tower	Any very tall building or structure.
trace	Evidence of a prior existence.
tramping	Walking a long time over difficult terrain.
tranquil	Calm or peaceful.
transact	To exchange or trade, as of ideas, money, goods, etc.
transparent	See-through; clear; allowing light to pass through almost undisturbed.
treading	Stepping, walking, or trampling.
treble	Any high-pitched or shrill voice or sound.
tremble	To shake, quiver, or vibrate.
trough	A long, narrow container, open on top, for feeding or watering animals.
tune	A song.
turbidly	With muddiness.
twilight	The period between daylight and darkness.
twined	Twisted or wound around.
unchangeable	Not able to be changed.
unto	Up to the time or degree that; until; till.
untrue	Not true; False.
uphill	Up a slope, toward higher ground.
vacant	Empty; unoccupied.
vain	Pointless, hopeless, or futile.
vainly	Conceitedly or overly proud of oneself.
vair	Fur from a squirrel with a black back and white belly.
vanished	Disappeared or became invisible.

Word	Definition
vapours (vapors)	Mists, steam or fumes suspended in the air.
vast	Very large or wide.
vault	Any arched ceiling or roof.
venturing	The act of one who takes a risky or daring journey.
Venus	The Roman goddess of love, beauty, and natural productivity.
vexing	Tossing back and forth; agitating; disquieting.
vile	Morally low; base; despicable.
virtue	1. Good moral conduct. 2. A creature embodying divine power, specifically one of the orders of heavenly beings.
visible	Able to be seen.
vision	Something imaginary one thinks one sees.
vital	Life-giving.
wafts	Floats gently through the air.
wailful	Sorrowful; mournful.
wards	The ridges on the inside of a lock.
waste	Gradual loss.
wastebasket	A small, indoor container for trash.
wayfarers	Travelers, especially on foot.
wearied	Tired; fatigued.
weathercock (weather-cock)	A weather vane, often in the form of a young male chicken.
wherein	Where, or in which location.
whippoorwill	A nocturnal insectivorous bird named for its call (whip-poor-will).
whir	To move or vibrate with a buzzing sound.
wide	Having a large physical extent from side to side.
wind	The act of winding or turning; a turn; a bend; a twist.
winnowing	Tossing about by blowing.
withdrew	Pulled back or away.
wobbling	Teetering back and forth.
woes	Great sadness or distress.
worth	Having value of; deserving of.
wrought	Having been worked or prepared somehow.
yea	Yes.

REFERENCES AND ADDITIONAL READING

1. *Emily Dickinson Poem "I'm Nobody"* (1891, {PD-US})
   a. Dickinson, E. (1891). "Poems by Emily Dickinson". Boston: Roberts Brothers. (Higginson, T. W. & Todd, Mabel Loomis, ed.)
   b. License: This work is in the public domain in the United States because it was published (or registered with the U.S. Copyright Office) before January 1, 1923.
2. *Emily Dickinson Poem "Hope is the Thing with Feathers"* (1891, {PD-US})
   a. a. Dickinson, E. (1891). "Poems by Emily Dickinson". Boston: Roberts Brothers. (Higginson, T. W. & Todd, Mabel Loomis, ed.)
   b. License: This work is in the public domain in the United States because it was published (or registered with the U.S. Copyright Office) before January 1, 1923.
3. *Emily Dickinson Poem "The Chariot"* (1890, {PD-US})
   a. Dickinson, E. (1890). "Poems by Emily Dickinson". Boston: Roberts Brothers. (Higginson, T. W. & Todd, Mabel Loomis, ed.)
   b. License: This work is in the public domain in the United States because it was published (or registered with the U.S. Copyright Office) before January 1, 1923.
4. *Emily Dickinson Poem "By the Sea"* (1891, {PD-US})
   a. Dickinson, E. (1891). "Poems by Emily Dickinson". Boston: Roberts Brothers. (Higginson, T. W. & Todd, Mabel Loomis, ed.)
   b. License: This work is in the public domain in the United States because it was published (or registered with the U.S. Copyright Office) before January 1, 1923.
5. *Robert Frost Poem "After Apple Picking"* (1915, {PD-US})
   a. Frost, R. (1915). "North of Boston". New York: Henry Holt and Company. 2nd ed.
   b. License: This work is in the public domain in the United States because it was published (or registered with the U.S. Copyright Office) before January 1, 1923.
6. *Robert Frost Poem "Ghost House"* (1915, {PD-US})
   a. Frost, R. (1915). "A boy's will". New York: Henry Holt and Company.
   b. License: This work is in the public domain in the United States because it was published (or registered with the U.S. Copyright Office) before January 1, 1923.
7. *Robert Frost Poem "October"* (1915, {PD-US})
   a. Frost, R. (1915). "A boy's will". New York: Henry Holt and Company.
   b. License: This work is in the public domain in the United States because it was published (or registered with the U.S. Copyright Office) before January 1, 1923.
8. *Robert Frost Poem "The Lockless Door"* (1920, {PD-US})
   a. Frost, R. (1920). "Miscellaneous Poems to 1920". New York: Henry Holt and Company.
   b. License: This work is in the public domain in the United States because it was published (or registered with the U.S. Copyright Office) before January 1, 1923.
9. *Henry Wadsworth Longfellow Poem "Haunted Houses"* (1893, {PD-US})
   a. Longfellow, H.W. (1893). "The Complete Poetical Works of Henry Wadsworth Longfellow". Boston and New York: Houghton, Mifflin & Co.
   b. License: This work is in the public domain in the United States because it was published (or registered with the U.S. Copyright Office) before January 1, 1923.
10. *Henry Wadsworth Longfellow Poem "Paul Revere's Ride"* (1909–14, {PD-US})
    a. Longfellow, H.W. (1909–14). "English Poetry III: From Tennyson to Whitman. Vol. XLII. The Harvard Classics". New York: P.F. Collier & Son.
    b. License: This work is in the public domain in the United States because it was published (or registered with the U.S. Copyright Office) before January 1, 1923.

11. *Henry Wadsworth Longfellow Poem "The Tide Rises, the Tide Falls"* **(1900, {PD-US})**
    a. Longfellow, H.W. (1900). "Stedman, Edmund Clarence, ed. An American Anthology, 1787–1900". Boston: Houghton Mifflin.
    b. License: This work is in the public domain in the United States because it was published (or registered with the U.S. Copyright Office) before January 1, 1923.
12. *Henry Wadsworth Longfellow Poem "Snow-flakes"* **(1904, {PD-US})**
    a. Longfellow, H.W. (1904). "The World's Best Poetry". Philadelphia: John D. Morris & Co.
    b. License: This work is in the public domain in the United States because it was published (or registered with the U.S. Copyright Office) before January 1, 1923.
13. *Paul Laurence Dunbar Poem "We Wear the Mask"* **(1896, {PD-US})**
    a. Dunbar, P.L. (1896). "Lyrics of Lowly Life". New York: Dodd, Mead, and Company.
    b. License: This work is in the public domain in the United States because it was published (or registered with the U.S. Copyright Office) before January 1, 1923.
14. *Paul Laurence Dunbar Poem "The Seedling"* **(1913, {PD-US})**
    a. Dunbar, P.L. (1913). "The Complete Poems of Paul Laurence Dunbar". New York: Dodd, Mead, and Company.
    b. License: This work is in the public domain in the United States because it was published (or registered with the U.S. Copyright Office) before January 1, 1923.
15. *Paul Laurence Dunbar Poem "Sunset"* **(1913, {PD-US})**
    a. Dunbar, P.L. (1913). "The Complete Poems of Paul Laurence Dunbar". New York: Dodd, Mead, and Company.
    b. License: This work is in the public domain in the United States because it was published (or registered with the U.S. Copyright Office) before January 1, 1923.
16. *Paul Laurence Dunbar Poem "He Had His Dream"* **(1913, {PD-US})**
    a. Dunbar, P.L. (1913). "The Complete Poems of Paul Laurence Dunbar". New York: Dodd, Mead, and Company.
    b. License: This work is in the public domain in the United States because it was published (or registered with the U.S. Copyright Office) before January 1, 1923.
17. *Christina Rossetti Poem "A Birthday"* **(1906, {PD-US})**
    a. Rossetti, C. (1906). "Poems". Boston: Little, Brown, and Company.
    b. License: This work is in the public domain in the United States because it was published (or registered with the U.S. Copyright Office) before January 1, 1923.
18. *Christina Rossetti Poem "Uphill"* **(1906, {PD-US})**
    a. Rossetti, C. (1906). "Poems". Boston: Little, Brown, and Company.
    b. License: This work is in the public domain in the United States because it was published (or registered with the U.S. Copyright Office) before January 1, 1923.
19. *Christina Rossetti Poem "The Queen of Hearts"* **(1906, {PD-US})**
    a. Rossetti, C. (1906). "Poems". Boston: Little, Brown, and Company.
    b. License: This work is in the public domain in the United States because it was published (or registered with the U.S. Copyright Office) before January 1, 1923.
20. *Christina Rossetti Poem "Summer"* **(1906, {PD-US})**
    a. Rossetti, C. (1906). "Poems". Boston: Little, Brown, and Company.
    b. License: This work is in the public domain in the United States because it was published (or registered with the U.S. Copyright Office) before January 1, 1923.
21. *Amy Lowell Poem "The Travelling Bear"* **(1915, {PD-US})**
    a. Lowell, A. et. al. (1915). "Some Imagist Poets – An Anthology". Boston and New York: Houghton Mifflin Company.
    b. License: This work is in the public domain in the United States because it was published (or registered with the U.S. Copyright Office) before January 1, 1923.

22. *Amy Lowell Poem "To a Friend"* (1912, {PD-US})
    a. Lowell, A. (1912). "A Dome of Many-Coloured Glass". Boston and New York: Houghton Mifflin Company.
    b. License: This work is in the public domain in the United States because it was published (or registered with the U.S. Copyright Office) before January 1, 1923.
23. *Amy Lowell Poem "Venus Transiens"* (1915, {PD-US})
    a. Lowell, A. et. al. (1915). "Some Imagist Poets – An Anthology". Boston and New York: Houghton Mifflin Company.
    b. License: This work is in the public domain in the United States because it was published (or registered with the U.S. Copyright Office) before January 1, 1923.
24. *Amy Lowell Poem "Winter's Turning"* (1919, {PD-US})
    a. Lowell, A. (1919). "Pictures of the Turning World". New York: The MacMillan Company.
    b. License: This work is in the public domain in the United States because it was published (or registered with the U.S. Copyright Office) before January 1, 1923.
25. *John Keats Poem "Bright Star, would I were steadfast as thou art"* (1875, {PD-US})
    a. Palgrave, Francis T., ed. (1875). "The Golden Treasury". London: Macmillan.
    b. License: This work is in the public domain in the United States because it was published (or registered with the U.S. Copyright Office) before January 1, 1923.
26. *John Keats Poem "Ode to Autumn"* (1875, {PD-US})
    a. Palgrave, Francis T., ed. (1875). "The Golden Treasury". London: Macmillan.
    b. License: This work is in the public domain in the United States because it was published (or registered with the U.S. Copyright Office) before January 1, 1923.
27. *John Keats Poem "On the Grasshopper and the Cricket"* (1884, {PD-US})
    a. Keats, J. (1884). "Poetical Works". London: Macmillan.
    b. License: This work is in the public domain in the United States because it was published (or registered with the U.S. Copyright Office) before January 1, 1923.
28. *John Keats Poem "To Sleep"* (1919, {PD-US})
    a. Quiller-Couch, Arthur Thomas, Sir. (1919). "The Oxford Book of English Verse". Oxford: Clarendon.
    b. License: This work is in the public domain in the United States because it was published (or registered with the U.S. Copyright Office) before January 1, 1923.
29. *Walt Whitman Poem "A Noiseless Patient Spider"* (1900, {PD-US})
    a. Whitman, Walt. (1900). "Leaves of Grass". Philadelphia: David McKay.
    b. License: This work is in the public domain in the United States because it was published (or registered with the U.S. Copyright Office) before January 1, 1923.
30. *Walt Whitman Poem "Longings for Home"* (1900, {PD-US})
    a. Whitman, Walt. (1900). "Leaves of Grass". Philadelphia: David McKay.
    b. License: This work is in the public domain in the United States because it was published (or registered with the U.S. Copyright Office) before January 1, 1923.
31. *Walt Whitman Poem "Night on the Prairies"* (1900, {PD-US})
    a. Whitman, Walt. (1900). "Leaves of Grass". Philadelphia: David McKay.
    b. License: This work is in the public domain in the United States because it was published (or registered with the U.S. Copyright Office) before January 1, 1923.
32. *Walt Whitman Poem "Pioneers! O Pioneers!"* (1900, {PD-US})
    a. Whitman, Walt. (1900). "Leaves of Grass". Philadelphia: David McKay.
    b. License: This work is in the public domain in the United States because it was published (or registered with the U.S. Copyright Office) before January 1, 1923.
33. *Elizabeth Barrett Browning Poem "How Do I Love Thee?"* (1909-1914, {PD-US})
    a. "English Poetry II: From Collins to Fitzgerald. Vol. XLI." The Harvard Classics. New York: P.F. Collier & Son, 1909–14.
    b. License: This work is in the public domain in the United States because it was published (or registered with the U.S. Copyright Office) before January 1, 1923.

34. *Elizabeth Barrett Browning Poem "The Best Thing in the World"* (1917, {PD-US})
    a. Warner, Charles Dudley, et al. "Library of World's Best Literature". New York: Warner Library Co., 1917.
    b. License: This work is in the public domain in the United States because it was published (or registered with the U.S. Copyright Office) before January 1, 1923.
35. *Elizabeth Barrett Browning Poem "A Musical Instrument"* (1895, {PD-US})
    a. Stedman, Edmund Clarence, ed. A Victorian Anthology, 1837–1895. Cambridge: Riverside Press, 1895.
    b. License: This work is in the public domain in the United States because it was published (or registered with the U.S. Copyright Office) before January 1, 1923.
36. *Elizabeth Barrett Browning Poem "Change Upon Change"* (1851, {PD-US})
    a. Barrett Browning, E. "Prometheus Bound, and other poems." New York: P.F. C.S. Francis & Co., 1851.
    b. License: This work is in the public domain in the United States because it was published (or registered with the U.S. Copyright Office) before January 1, 1923.
37. *Map of Europe* ({PD-US})
    a. Source: https://commons.wikimedia.org/wiki/File:Europe_geopolitical_map_of_Europe.jpg
    b. License: This work has been released into the public domain by its author, *Public Domain Images*. This applies worldwide. *Public Domain Images* grants anyone the right to use this work for any purpose, without any conditions, unless such conditions are required by law.
38. *Map of the United States* ({PD-US})
    a. Source: https://commons.wikimedia.org/wiki/File:United_States_Public_Domain_Map.svg
    b. License: This image is a work of a United States Department of Justice employee, taken or made as part of that person's official duties. As a work of the U.S. federal government, the image is in the public domain (17 U.S.C. § 101 and 105).
39. *Emily Dickinson Picture* (circa 1846-1847, {PD-US})
    a. Source: https://commons.wikimedia.org/wiki/File:Black-white_photograph_of_Emily_Dickinson_(Restored).jpg
    b. License: This media file is in the public domain in the United States. This applies to U.S. works where the copyright has expired, often because its first publication occurred prior to January 1, 1923.
40. *Robert Frost Picture* (1913, {PD-US})
    a. Source: https://commons.wikimedia.org/wiki/File:Robert_Frost,_1913.JPG
    b. License: This media file is in the public domain in the United States. This applies to U.S. works where the copyright has expired, often because its first publication occurred prior to January 1, 1923.
41. *Paul Laurence Dunbar Picture* (1906, {PD-US})
    a. Source: https://commons.wikimedia.org/wiki/File:Paul_Laurence_Dunbar_cph.3a46805.jpg
    b. License: This media file is in the public domain in the United States. This applies to U.S. works where the copyright has expired, often because its first publication occurred prior to January 1, 1923.
42. *Christina Rossetti Portrait* (1866, {PD-US})
    a. Source: https://commons.wikimedia.org/wiki/File:Christina_Rossetti_2.jpg
    b. License: This media file is in the public domain in the United States. This applies to U.S. works where the copyright has expired, often because its first publication occurred prior to January 1, 1923. The author died in 1882, so this work is in the public domain in its country of origin and other countries and areas where the copyright term is the author's life plus 100 years or less.
43. *Amy Lowell Picture* (1925, {PD-US})
    a. Source: https://commons.wikimedia.org/wiki/File:TIME_Magazine_cover_from_March_2,_1925_featuring_Amy_Lowell.jpg
    b. License: This work is in the public domain because it was published in the United States between 1923 and 1963 and although there may or may not have been a copyright notice, the copyright was not renewed. Unless its author has been dead for the required period, it is copyrighted in the countries or areas that do not apply the rule of the shorter term for US works.

44. *John Keats Portrait* by William Hilton (circa 1822, {PD-US})
    a. Source: https://commons.wikimedia.org/wiki/File:John_Keats_by_William_Hilton.jpg
    b. License: This work is in the public domain in its country of origin and other countries and areas where the copyright term is the author's life plus 100 years or less. This media file is in the public domain in the United States. This applies to U.S. works where the copyright has expired, often because its first publication occurred prior to January 1, 1923.
45. *Walt Whitman Picture* (circa 1855-1865, {PD-US})
    a. Source: https://commons.wikimedia.org/wiki/File:Walt_Whitman_-_Brady-Handy.jpg
    b. License: This media file is in the public domain in the United States. This applies to U.S. works where the copyright has expired, often because its first publication occurred prior to January 1, 1923. This work is in the public domain in its country of origin and other countries and areas where the copyright term is the author's life plus 100 years or less.
46. *Elizabeth Barrett Browning Picture* (1859, {PD-US})
    a. Source: https://commons.wikimedia.org/wiki/File:Elizabeth-Barrett-Browning,_Poetical_Works_Volume_I,_engraving.png
    b. License: This media file is in the public domain in the United States. This applies to U.S. works where the copyright has expired, often because its first publication occurred prior to January 1, 1923. This work is in the public domain in its country of origin and other countries and areas where the copyright term is the author's life plus 100 years or less.
47. *Emily Dickinson*. Wikipedia. Wikipedia.org. n.p.
48. *Robert Frost*. Wikipedia. Wikipedia.org. n.p.
49. *Henry Wadsworth Longfellow*. Wikipedia. Wikipedia.org. n.p.
50. *Paul Laurence Dunbar*. Wikipedia. Wikipedia.org. n.p.
51. *Christina Rossetti*. Wikipedia. Wikipedia.org. n.p.
52. *Amy Lowell*. Wikipedia. Wikipedia.org. n.p.
53. *John Keats*. Wikipedia. Wikipedia.org. n.p.
54. *Walt Whitman*. Wikipedia. Wikipedia.org. n.p.
55. *Elizabeth Barrett Browning*. Wikipedia. Wikipedia.org. n.p.
56. *All Other Clipart and Images*. Open Clipart. openclipart.org. n.p. ({PD-US})
57. *All Definitions*. Wiktionary: Public Domain Sources. en.wiktionary.org. n.p. ({PD-US})

ABOUT THE AUTHOR

Sonja Glumich is a scientist, educator, wife, and mother who is inspired by Charlotte Mason's living works approach to homeschooling. She is the founder of Under the Home (underthehome.org), an online homeschool curriculum featuring low-cost courses in art history, poetry, prose, music, history, science, studio art, mathematics, reading, and Shakespeare. Sonja's husband, Chris, homeschools their three school-aged children using the Under the Home curriculum as featured in this book.

Sonja graduated magna cum laude with bachelor's degrees in biology, chemistry, and computer science and later earned a master's degree in information technology. She has also completed education classes and student teaching leading to certification to teach secondary science.

Sonja has experience teaching students of all ages, from preschool to graduate school, including as a middle school and high school science public school teacher. She has also served as an Adjunct Professor for Syracuse University and co-created two graduate-level cyber courses. She currently works as a computer scientist for the Air Force Research Laboratory. Her current research and education interests are security systems engineering, cyber vulnerability assessments, and everything homeschooling.

www.ingramcontent.com/pod-product-compliance
Lightning Source LLC
LaVergne TN
LVHW081356060426
835510LV00016B/1867